THE CHRISTIAN
as a
JOURNALIST

the HADDAM HOUSE *series on*

The Christian in His Vocation

EDWARD LEROY LONG, JR.

series editor

The Christian as a Doctor

JAMES T. STEPHENS AND

EDWARD LEROY LONG, JR.

Christianity and the Scientist

IAN G. BARBOUR

The Christian as a Journalist

RICHARD T. BAKER

THE CHRISTIAN

as a

JOURNALIST

by RICHARD T. BAKER

ASSOCIATION PRESS   NEW YORK

Preface

The work of the journalist, and particularly that of the newspaper reporter, is not commonly considered a religious calling. But if the Reformation doctrine that all legitimate earthly tasks can be undertaken from divine compulsion is correct, then indeed the work of the journalist is no exception. And, if the thesis of this book is right, not only can the place of the newsman in the divine scheme of things be conceded—it can be affirmed and acknowledged with zeal and in depth.

The approach of this volume is one of encounter and search, as well as affirmation. The book takes the form of a conversation with a person entering upon a career in journalism, particularly the beginning reporter. As such it undoubtedly reflects the fact that the author is in daily communication with the student set and young professionals. Those who read this book, whether in the profession or

5

not, should profit from overhearing the conversation. In re-
viewing the problems that are confronted in journalism
—philosophical, systemic, functional, personal, and psycho-
logical—the author seeks for the kind of understanding that
leads a step nearer toward a solution of such difficulties. But
the book is not presumed to be thick with answers and solu-
tions, nor indeed should it be. Only by a process of tough
wrestling with the realities of life do the fibers of men get
toughened or the purposes of God get served.

The author of this volume likes journalism. He thinks it
is a noble calling. He thinks it is a divine calling. He does
not ignore the faults, yet finds many things in journalism, as
he knows it, full of rewards and satisfactions. He takes his
stand with the philosophers of freedom and he is delighted
that Milton, Locke, Zenger, and Tom Paine touched the history of his profession. He loves his government, but he is
happy that it doesn't own and operate the press. He would
rather work for a business-owned press in Podunk, U.S.A.,
than for the party press of France or the state press of Moscow. He thinks distortions, malproportions, and sensationalism in the news are the prices one pays for freedom, and
that more intelligent and responsible readers and editors
will provide the best available corrective for abuse. He
thinks that modern journalistic coverage, the mass of facts,
is phenomenal, that no generation ever had a broader, more
detailed picture of its age, though he does not say that the
coverage is complete or that the mass of facts doesn't need to
be interpreted and related to the broader issues of our time
or composed into sharper delineations of the truth. He thinks
that the press is a potent force in society, and a force for
good, but he does not make of it a sacred cow beyond all
criticism.

Journalism is one of the most public of all callings, and everybody has an interest in it. The public is possessive about the journalist's profession—everybody feels he can edit his newspaper better than those who do it. The general reader should therefore be ready to participate vicariously in the encounter here portrayed of the journalist with the realities of his job. It will help him to read his newspaper more wisely, co-operate in cases of necessity with giving news more adequately, and rally to the defense of the free press as a guardian of the democratic heritage and a faithful servant of a chastened and enriched culture. The journalist who threads through his task with the self-critical allegiance to his work that is called for in these pages, like the truest pilgrims in any faith, will serve God in his daily work and inspire his fellow men to the same maturity of life that he nobly portrays.

EDWARD LeROY LONG, JR.
Series Editor

Contents

Chapter		*Page*
	Preface by Edward LeRoy Long, Jr.	5
One	In the Beginning . . . the Word	13

Journalism—seemingly secular . . . The sanctity of words . . . No community without communication . . . The journalist—an historian . . . Recording human crises . . . In tune with reality

| Two | The Goal of the Enterprise . . . Truth . . . . | 26 |

The pursuit of truth . . . From truth to freedom . . . Truth—only relative . . . Watching your bias . . . Current history—a morality play . . . Perversions in the journalist's role . . . Public morality . . . Why journalism deals with holy things

| Three | The Ambiguous Base . . . Freedom . . . . | 41 |

Problems of a free press . . . The power of truth . . . Freedom—a paradoxical thing . . . Necessary curbs on freedom . . . "A clear and present danger" . . . A cause of international disagreements . . . A press too free? . . . Possible controls over excessive freedom . . . Responsibility—a precondition of freedom

Chapter   *Page*

Four   In the System ... Questions   59

> A merchant-minded press ... Dependence on ad-
> vertisers ... But if there were no advertisers? ...
> Monopoly ownership—a potential danger ... The
> safeguard of other competitive media ... Journal-
> ism—a paying job ... Situations that will trouble
> you ... Journalism and your personal life

Five   In the Process ... Difficulties   75

> Frustrations of your high purposes ... Communi-
> cations—an unfinished business ... Limitation of
> space—a constant ... Limitation of time ... Prob-
> lems in journalistic style ... "Off-the-record" ma-
> terial ... Obstacles on the road to truth ... Retro-
> active extras

Six   From the Endeavor ... Authenticity   93

> Always the viewer of history ... "The fourth es-
> tate" ... Reporters objective, politicians subjective
> ... Conflict of interest—a danger ... To accept or
> not to accept gifts? ... Exploiting the emotions
> ... Motivations in journalists ... Journalism—no
> second-choice calling

Seven   At the End ... a Word   115

> Standards of excellence—not enough ... Even
> the truth—not enough ... An instrument for a
> more just society ... "What do ye more than
> others?"

        Notes by Chapter   121

THE CHRISTIAN

as a

JOURNALIST

CHAPTER ONE

In the Beginning ... the Word

The day you report for work in journalism, you will not be struck with overtones of piety in the place. Your associates, behind their gruff exteriors, will ring true to the cliché and have hearts of gold—good men, serious and dedicated. Professional standards will be frequently mentioned and taken seriously. You will see efficient procedures and hear a lot of alert, knowledgeable comment. You will feel excitement. You will sense a high degree of public responsibility.

Journalism—Seemingly Secular

But, all in all, you will not find the temples of journalistic activity exactly reeking with the incenses of sanctity. There will be no morning devotions as reporters, editors, and broadcasters march out to serve the Lord in their daily lives and work. References to the Deity will be heard frequently, but not in the context of worship and praise. Journalism, in all its forms, places its functionaries so close to the raw edges of current history that you will tend to find yourself steeped in the attitudes of doubt and unbelief. Yours is a secular world, often sordid and profane.

Trailing a narcotics peddler through the city playground, taking notes that turn your stomach at the trial of a rapist-killer—are these the ways to serve your God and fellow man? Is there any religious meaning in the life of a journalist, any ethical meaning? Does God call anybody to this kind of vocation?

The answer to all these questions has to be yes. The man who stands on the communications bridge, seeing, observing, telling man the story of himself, is one of God's most prized servants. Perhaps it's an ugly story, perhaps the journalist's world appears possessed by evil. Nevertheless, the journalist's work is a vocation, a response to a divine call, a coming to attention before commands that are for him absolute and ultimate.

Few journalists would state the case in just this way. They are so preoccupied with the immediate and the momentary that they are disinclined to be philosophical. They are not ones to hold their work in far perspective. Yet they would not be journalists if they did not believe that there was meaning in the unfolding journal of human life. To dedicate one's life and talents to finding meaning in history is to assume that meaning is there. This assumption so deeply underlies the work of the journalist that it seldom gets stated. But it is the ultimate ground upon which he works, and ultimates are religious, and response to ultimates takes the nature of religious commitment.

The Sanctity of Words

Words are the journalist's basic tools. When the fishing fleet goes out of Gloucester in the early summer, the vessels take positions in the harbor and are blessed. The tools of the fisherman's craft thus become consecrated—though many would say the boats are better consecrated by the daily duty of the men than by the specific ritual of the priests. Few writers pack their dictionaries off to church to have the tools of their craft sanctified. Yet, in a curious sense, words—these minimal tools of the journalist—are sanctified.

In his delightful essay on style that appears as the closing chapter of *The Elements of Style*,* [1] E. B. White writes: "If one is to write, one must believe—in the truth and worth of the scrawl. . . ." These are strong words that Mr. White is using—"believe," "truth," "worth."

The sanctity of words, "the truth and worth of the scrawl," was obviously clear to the Judaeo-Christian ancients whose memorials are preserved in the Bible. The idea of the Word, the priority of language—these are insistent biblical themes. Others can supply the precise exegesis of St. John's idea of the *Logos;* here it is enough to call attention to the existence of it. Why did John take the prologue space to his Gospel to write a poem about the *Logos*, the Word? What was he trying to say, to affirm? What religious truth was he announcing?

Obviously, the apostrophe to the Word was intended to back up his chronicle to its original beginnings in creation. "In the beginning was the Word, and the Word was with God, and the Word was God." The passage has strong hints

* All numbered references appear under "Notes by Chapter" at the end of the book.

within it that turn the pages back to the first passages in the
book of Genesis. And, turning there, we find another strange
apostrophe to the Word. Each of the acts of creation is introduced by a simple line: "And God said, . . ." The act of
verbalizing obviously had some strong religious meaning to
these writers. Perhaps a fascination with the gift of language. Perhaps some insight into the inseparability of personality and verbalization. The symbols of truth that are
struggling for expression here are related to personal Mind
and Will, to the mind's powers of logical conception, to
the fact that precedent to all details of history are the con-
cepts that emerge in utterance. "And God said, . . ." This was
the beginning Word.

Another set of writers might have told the story differ-
ently, accenting different points, affirming different aspects
of the same truth. They might have had God moving the
nebulae, fusing hydrogen atoms, stirring the germ of life
from the sea. They might, and that's their business. The
interesting thing is that the Bible affirmed the truth in a
different way. It began in the beginning with God and his
utterance.

Utterance is the business of journalism, and utterance is
originally divine. Not everything that journalism utters is
divinely inspired by God. There are other bylines in the
newspapers and other commentators on the air. But the fact
that mind shall conceive and bear fruit in utterance is a fact
that has original religious significance. It is in this sense that
the journalist, as he engages in his craft, partakes of certain
holy elements, endowed with blessedness from the moment of creation. You do believe in the Word, or you are
no journalist.

No Community Without Communication

There is another sense in which the Word is sanctified. It is a primary instrument of community. In fact, the noun "communication" shows its dependence as a word upon the idea of community. This is a way of saying something that every woman has always known: when two persons get together they talk. Language is the first instrument of interpersonal and intergroup relations. Whatever bonds of understanding exist to hold men together are bonds of communicative words, all the way from a baby's first cry in his mother's ear to the United Nations charter. There is no community without communication.

At times you will feel very sorry for yourself and moan about your inarticulateness; nobody understands you. It is undoubtedly true that human minds never quite really meet. But you can't make an hypothesis for life out of that. Persons are interrelated in too many ways. The fact of community is too real. Would anyone argue seriously that community was a thing to be despised, that community was not blessed and intended by God? Take your authorities where you will—historians, sociologists, psychologists, political scientists, the together-tethered editors of *McCall's*— and you will not get much argument about the necessity for interpersonal compacts for living. Jesus said as much in making love the basic compulsion of life.

Men stand under divine orders to cleave together. Anyone who adds one ounce of mortar to the structure of community runs an errand for God. The divine imperative on the communicators within community is so insistent that it hurts. The users of language are the first principals in establishing community. Philologists will tell you in fascinat-

ing detail that the most intimate history of a people is reflected in its language. The subtleties of its moods, the
proofs of what it holds most dear, the signs of its taboos and
hates—study its language and you study a people. Because
of this priority of language in the community, you begin to
sense again a kind of sacred responsibility that rests upon
anyone who functions with the language in a community.

Communication is a sacred act because it is the way God
acts with his community. You can't begin to count the number of times the biblical record has God *speaking* to his people. "And God said unto Abraham . . . unto Moses . . . unto
Isaiah. . . ." The majestic reading of the Decalogue begins:
"And God spoke all these words, saying, I am the Lord thy
God. . . ." It is beautiful as literature, perhaps rather crude
and anthropomorphic as a factual story. The interesting
thing, however, is that the God of the Bible, for all his distance, elevation, transcendent otherness, is a God in constant dialogue with his people. You may not believe a word
of what he says, you may find very unsophisticated some of
the topics of conversation between this people and their
God. But you can not escape the fundamental truth that is
being affirmed: communication is very clearly a mark of the
human-divine relation that the Bible is talking about.

Prayer is another demonstration from the Judaeo-Christian tradition of the sacredness of communication. God's
love for man and man's love for God find their most immediate expression in discourse.

Equally, man's love for man, this initial thrust that forms
all human community, finds its most immediate expression
in verbal communication. If you're going into journalism,
you carry this responsibility of handling very elemental
things, of dealing with forces that begin where community

begins, and of behaving yourself accordingly. Fidelity to the truth, respect for your reader, clarity, respect for the language—all these things become much more than prudent virtues; they become compulsions that bind you with supreme, divine authority.

A trivial example: You write your first news story when you go to work in journalism about a house party given by the Abner P. Dieffenbacherheims. The next day a telephone call informs you in somewhat acid tones that the Abner P. Dieffenbacherheims are, correctly, the Diefenbacherheims, and the initial is B., and Mr. Diefenbacherheim's mother christened him Ambrose. So you misspelled a name? For an extra "f" all the kingdoms of journalism are lost? It was only a house party anyway. Go ahead, make all the excuses you want. Your real offense was breaking a trust that bound you to behave faithfully. You were the communicator in society, and into the communication stream you poured error, you broke the bonds of mutual respect that are the hoops of steel tying society together. Perhaps the town will not fall apart on your error, your carelessness, your infidelity to the community. It was, after all, only a small sin. But the point is that it was a sin, an infraction of laws of life that govern with the force of God behind them.

Jessamyn West writes in her book, *To See the Dream* [2]: "It's a risky affair, writing, and can never be played close to the chest, hiding everything which may give you away. That's what writing is—giving yourself away." Communication is the beginning of the process of losing yourself to find yourself.

No one goes into journalism and makes a satisfying life for himself who does not go by faith—in the supreme worth of the Word and in the supreme worth of communication.

The Journalist—an Historian

The vocation of journalist fits the divine plan in another way, and that has to do with the subject matter he handles. In essence, a journalist is an historian. He focuses his attention on the immediate, the contemporary, the current, but it is history all the same. He lives on the leading edge of history, watching and observing and telling what he sees, moving it back in a steady stream into record. His fascination with all that transpires on the front edge of human history is enormous, his curiosity insatiable. There is something devout in the response of the journalist to all that happens to men and among men in the present tense. Something devout. He is responding by faith.

His fascination, his curiosity, his approaches, his routines, all declare an underlying belief about human history that it is real, valuable, meaningful. You don't spend all the energy that journalists spend in microscopic attention to the minutes of each day's meetings without revealing your values and your beliefs. It is clear that where your treasure is, your heart is, also.

 Your devotion to human history, as a journalist, brings you close to understanding something central and fundamental about religious truth as the Judaeo-Christian traditions have declared it. Judaism and Christianity have been called "historical" religions. This does not mean that they once took place in history, and then stopped. It means that for them, history is never unimportant, that God's purposes run through it, that not even sparrows fall without God's noticing and caring.

You can find religions that get their deepest meanings by bursting out of history, or by leaving it alone to run on its own dynamics, or by obscuring the moral values within it. Judaeo-Christian belief permits of none of these detours around the importance of history. Nor does the journalist dare to leave history alone. In his basic assumptions about the reality of the event in time and space, the journalist is embraced within an "historical" religion.

Recording Human Crises

A time-honored formula—another bit of the folklore of American journalism—for operating a successful newspaper is to print the news of people who are "hatched, matched and dispatched." It is probably a little minimal, this formula, but you can go quite a distance in journalism on the news of births, marriages, deaths. This formula is mentioned to call attention to a place at which the interests of journalism and religion coincide. The reporter's notebook comes out at the word of births, weddings, and deaths—three exact points in human history when the priest comes out, also. The church endows birth, marriage, and death with sacramental significance. Religion stands ready to bless these critical moments in human life.

We have seen that the journalist shares in a religious mission as his eye sweeps across the whole panorama of current history. It is even more true that he is religiously sent into his daily work when you consider that his practiced eye is picking out on the human scene those points that are marked by crisis. The concern of the journalist for the human crisis is a concern that is identically shared by the ministries of religion. One of the definitions of "news" is this: an event in current history that varies from the normal, the regular, the usual. This definition puts the journalist continuously in the middle of the stream of the abnormal, the irregular, the unusual, the crisis moments of human history.

The church, in its role as priest and pastor, as comforter, as scourger of injustice, and in its final role as the agent for man's supreme fulfillment, is equally concerned for the crisis in men's lives. A trouble, an ill, accident and crime, injustice and pain, conflict and war—these constitute a catalogue of concerns that call both journalism and religion to attention. The church has been criticized for having lost much of its revolutionary vigor and sense of crisis. If it is too placid, normal, comfortable, perhaps the voices from journalism are prophet's voices to save the temple.

But Christianity, though it is one of the historical religions, is not completely so. This paradoxical fact may seem to raise doubts for the journalist. Can his calling ever be a completely orthodox Christian one? Don't answer that question yet. Let's have another look at this paradoxical attitude of Christianity toward history. For the Christian everything that takes place in history is critically important, but history can not be depended upon to fulfill itself finally. In other words, history is important, but not important ultimately. (This sounds like nonsense.) Men will struggle valiantly and significantly through the swamp of human history, but they will never achieve the mounts of perfection within history. There will be relative differences in all they do. Some struggles and victories will be more significant than others. Within history moral distinction will always be necessary. But, ultimately and absolutely, human history will not march happily forward to a perfect consummation on its own power. God finally makes history perfect by overruling it. Theologians will explain all this as the eschatological hope.

Whatever they call it, the truth is that Christianity is on the pessimistic side about history, over the long haul, and sees a rather bleak picture of tragedy within it. Is the journalist more optimistic? In his constant attention to the "glut of occurrences" does he tend to become fixed on them, and only them? How does one report superhistory, or an act from outside history, or an eschatological hope?

This illustration is probably stretched seven ways to fit this context, but read it anyway. It's a homely illustration to show that journalists do have a kind of eschatology. The biggest type in any printing shop, the blackest and boldest, as any printer will tell you, is seldom used. In an offhand, not particularly theological way he will tell you why. "We're saving that for the Second Coming." You've heard the comment. It's a revealing little piece of folklore that seems to say that even journalists, with all their infatuation over the passing parade, know that the biggest story of them all will be a story of something that happens *to* the parade, not in it.

Perhaps a journalist is naïve and optimistic about the course of human events, perhaps he is fatalistic about the forces that move through history, perhaps he sees no meaning in the stream, perhaps he sees too much meaning—these are all possible attitudes. They do not necessarily define journalism, however, as a calling in which one can not serve both God and man. Journalism has no built-in hostility to the Christian view of life. One can look upon his work in journalism as a ministry through which he glorifies God, works His purposes, and serves his fellow men.

In Tune with Reality

The journalist keeps the public in tune with reality. If it is true about man that he should understand history, have concerns within it, and draw moral distinctions within it, then journalism serves him well to make that understanding as accurate and detailed as possible, as broad as possible, as clear as possible, as soon as possible. As the journalist moves through his working day, noting and recording all the events, the thoughts and actions, the hard facts of what people are doing with themselves on earth, he amasses a tremendous volume of detail and throws it at his reader. It is a somewhat unsorted mass, photographic, "surfacey" and momentary.

The journalist has been criticized for the shallowness of his perspective, for his cult of immediacy and objectivity. The trend in modern reporting is responsive to those criticisms, and efforts are being made to probe more deeply, to interpret, to analyze, and to comment. The editorial writer and the columnist have always commented on the news, but most of them have won their spurs as accurate reporters. Comment is not possible without the raw material that the ordinary reporter must provide: the flat, photographic picture of the human situation.

This picture is not to be despised, although it is fashionable in some circles to scoff at the journalist as "thin," only a mirror, superficial. It really does not matter what goes into that picture, if it is accurate and properly proportioned. The better the picture, the sounder human knowledge and decision will be. And the reverse is true. Unless human knowledge is informed with the facts of existence, wishes begin to govern moral decision, whims substitute for law, and fantasy displaces reality. If the picture is not in line with reality, human knowledge swings between imagining life worse than it is to better than it is, and men are robbed of the basis for practical, ethical behavior. Anyone who can observe and report the data of existence, with the involvement necessary to sense it deeply and the aloofness necessary to perceive it in perspective, provides the original stuff out of which sounder human knowledge and decision come. In the beginning . . . the word.

CHAPTER TWO

The Goal of the Enterprise . . . Truth

As you think seriously about the goals and ideals of journalism, it is certain that you would define them in words not far from John 8:32 (RSV): ". . . you will know the truth, and the truth will make you free." You would speak of journalism's search for truth, and you would have something to say about freedom that blossoms from the root of truth. The practical goal of the serious journalist is to observe so closely, to bring to bear upon his subject so much relevant fact, to burrow so deeply and to communicate so clearly that he spreads among the people a true account of the event and moment in human history that he is covering.

The Pursuit of Truth

The day you twist your first fact you will notice tones of positive hostility as your editor gives you a short lecture on accuracy. Even if he does not lecture you, the damage is done. An inaccuracy has been written into history. You were the weak link in the chain of accurate communication that holds society together. There are little shrines and altars around a newspaper shop. You will find that journalism, by definition, is ultimately committed to the truth. It steers its daily course, however imperfectly, in line with the perfect principle that each day's chronicle shall be accurately, truthfully reflected.

Journalists have been accused of picturing life as sordid, ugly, wretched. Insofar as they have malproportioned the picture to emphasize the filth and ugliness, they are guilty as charged. But a picture that has had all the blue tones filtered out of it may make the so-called family newspaper; it also portrays a very dull family—a family absolutely unequipped to do anything in or about the history of which it is a part.

The issue at stake is not so much whether rosy hues or blue tints are most pleasing to the sensitivities. The issue at stake is the color of the picture as it stands, stark, real, dynamic, tender, and touched by both the hand of God and the clutch of men. The actors in the picture are real members of the human family, both creators of glory and victims of pathos. God has his eye on what happens to the human family. So does the journalist, who is under a divine compulsion to see the events correctly.

As a journalist you must think of the true account in the broadest sense. Without minor inaccuracies, of course, but more than that—you strive for an account that is so unobscured, so thorough, so crystal clear that when the reader reads he is in the presence of the truth, the whole truth, and nothing but the truth. For instance, as a reporter you write that "the Governor said today that his political opponent had been a black-shirted fascist under Mussolini." That is a true thing. Names spelled correctly. And the Governor said precisely what you the reporter have quoted him as saying. But you are not happy about letting this superficially true report stand, when you know that the object of the Governor's wrath has never been anything but a poor wheat farmer in Saskatchewan. You sense the difference between a true thing and the truth, and it is this larger truth that you seek to serve. Somewhere in your account the public must be told that the Governor was wrong, if the whole truth is to be there.

Yes, a chief pursuit of the conscientious journalist is the truth. Then he will likely go on to explain that he pursues the truth so faithfully in order to provide the raw data upon which free men in a free society can make the decisions that hold the society together. Joseph Pulitzer, when he was founding the school of journalism at Columbia University, wrote:

> While it is a great pleasure to feel that a large number of young men will be helped to a better start in life by means of this college, this is not my primary object. Neither is the elevation of the profession which I love so much and regard so highly. In all my planning the chief end I had in view was the welfare of the Republic. It will be the object of this college to make better journalists, who will make better newspapers, which will better serve the public. It will impart knowledge—not for its own sake, but to be used for the public service. It will try to develop character, but even that will be only a means to the one supreme end—the public good.

Almost every journalist would define his supreme end in the same way: accurate public information so that social action will be sound.

From Truth to Freedom

Does it seem strange to you that the clear aims and objectives of journalism come so close to a word spoken by Jesus nearly two thousand years ago? Is there any relation? Could Jesus—and John quoting him—have possibly had modern journalism in mind?

Probably not. So don't snatch at more than your share of biblical sanction for your calling. The fact is that the journalist's creed, these highest aims and ideals, stem more from the Renaissance and rationalism than they do from Jesus and John. They are, thus, more secular ideals than religious ones. They assume an ultimate worth for man's reason, that he is able by the light in his mind to get to the truth. They assume that truth is an achievable goal to be put together from the bottom up, the pieces being all the little true things that the seeking and the struggles and the clashes of men will produce. And they assume the basically optimistic proposition that when man's reason shall prevail and know the truth, peace and perfect order shall be the fruit. You will find in the journalism you practice that all these assumptions, all your assumptions, lead to a zealous belief in a democratic ideology. If the truth will make you free, the freedom you are talking about is pretty much summed up in the idea of free men in a free society, namely, democratic government.

Unfortunately, there are differences between all these assumptions about the truth and the truth that Jesus was talking about in John's record. Jesus was talking about the truth that came from commitment to him and the revelation of God's truth that was incarnate in him. He was really not talking about the truth that you grub around and find by yourself. The comment was part of an address to the Jews that had to do with their continuance in him, their commitment to him. A few words previously, he seemed to anticipate the age of rationalism, and said: "You are from below, I am from above; you are of this world, I am not of this world" (John 8:23). Apparently, the liberating truth of Jesus was much more a divine revelation than it was an achievement of reason.

Now, before you burn yourself at the stake for heresy, let us see where we are, where our ideals as journalists have led us. From the standpoint of the strict biblical perspective, the journalist's truth is a little muscle-bound in the head. Biblical truth is enriched by the insights of emotion and feeling, the understanding and appreciation of personality and relationship, by loyalty, commitment, and love, and by faith. But this is not to say that truth is ever unreasonable. Man has been endowed with rational powers, and he is expected to use them just as far as they will take him. There is nothing unbiblical about the exercise of a man's reason. As a steward of his talents, he is expected to use his reason faithfully, imaginatively, creatively, fruitfully. If you, as a journalist, have used your reason in pursuit of the truth about a human situation, and have acted to expose the truth for the public good, you have been involved in no heretical behavior. Your motive and your act have offended no divine plan.

Truth—Only Relative

Truth, as the Bible talks about it, is ultimate truth, and stands in judgment over all lesser truths and lesser goals. Truth, as you expose it, is subject to measurement against the ultimate. This means that the truth about a human situation, as you explore it carefully, shrewdly, and with all the best powers you can exercise, is still a relative truth, and only relative. The public good you hope to serve by your exposures of the truth is only relative. The social goal, even as it is defined as democratic government, is only relative.

But bear in mind that your truth and your goal may be relatively good, and should be passionately pursued. Just because you can approach the truth only relatively is no invitation to give up the approach and resign yourself to the pursuit of falsehood and bias. Just because your democratic goal can be only relatively achieved does not depreciate the value of your effort toward an informed public opinion in a free society. There are moral distinctions all along the relative scale between the false and the true. There are moral distinctions between any two types of social organization. Nothing that has been written here should be interpreted to belittle human reason, to obscure moral distinctions, or to devitalize anyone's efforts in behalf of truth or the public good.

The biblical view of truth should not be so hard for you to understand as a journalist. Rationalism, as a philosophical climate, is rather cool to the modern touch. The limits of reason, of reasonableness, of rationality are clearly sensed in this age of passions, change, complexity, and conflict. And a great deal of effort is expended in concocting rea-

sonable explanations of irrationality. You will know how
elusive is the truth. However relentlessly you pursue it—
covering a strike, or a town council meeting, or an African
independence movement—you will sense with anguish that
the whole truth keeps eluding you and is almost impossible
to communicate. The white light of reason doesn't seem to
have the wattage to penetrate the refractive nature of
human experience. You will know these frustrations; and,
hopefully, you will never let them get you down, because
it is still true, no matter how difficult the task, that journalism has a vocation from God to pursue the truth that makes
men free.

Watching Your Bias

All that the Bible said about faith and commitment as
access routes to the truth are realized with demonic twists
in the world we know today. A Soviet court, building a
structure of truth in a given case, produces a story colored
at all points by the loyalties of that court. What seems to be
true in Washington is not true in Havana. The balance sheet
of United States Steel is a neutral, observable, measurable
document. Yet it looks like one thing to the steel workers,
and like quite another thing to management. What seems
to be the truth about civil liberty in the Attorney General's
office is not the truth in a statehouse somewhere else, and is
something else again in Capetown, South Africa. Truth, as
Jesus said it would do when he called for commitment to
him, reveals itself to seekers in line with their fundamental
loyalties and faith.

This will worry you as a journalist. You will wonder
whether the truth you are communicating is your truth
only, or the real story. You will find yourself disturbed about

your own ideological bias. You will fear occasionally that it may be blinding you against your will (in fact, in no respect whatsoever to your will) to rich, clarifying avenues to the real truth. What is the true story about public opinion in China, the morale of the people, the consent of the governed? You would know better than to accept as true a report from the propaganda organs in Peiping. You would not ask a correspondent from Formosa to answer the questions for you. You could find reasons to suspect some bias in the reports of Reuters and Tass, or correspondents from India or Japan or Indonesia. How about you? Could you be sure of yourself? How ultimate are your commitments? How partial, how ideologically warped, how self-hypnotized is your view? Preconception is not alone a journalist's problem. Social scientists of all kinds, historians, and the public have their assumptions that color all they write and read and think. It is easy to indulge in a species of automatic writing, automatic thinking. One is automatically parochial, automatically liberal, automatically cynical, depending on who he is. The important thing for you, the journalist, is to examine your preconceptions, recognize them, and strive with all your might to reveal the truth that sets men free.

Current History—a Morality Play

The drama of current history is a morality play. A newspaper takes off after an official with his hand in the public till. A television documentary exposes the abuses of power of a United States Senator. A magazine, dramatically and persuasively, pleads for safety on the highways. Forces for good and forces for evil are at work in the human story, and the organs of journalism are day after day exposing those forces before the public eye.

This means that, in a sense, journalism is a moral judge of all that takes place on the front edge of history, and it finds itself again involved with vocational responsibilities as steward for the highest and best standards of social justice. It works under a call to do something about liberty and justice for all. Not only in his supreme beliefs, identifications, and purposes, but also as a moral agent, the journalist confesses his part in divine plans.

As a matter of fact, the journalist is obsessed by matters of moral significance. A case could even be made that he is a petty moralizer, an oversimplifier of moral struggles, an advocate of the ethics of black-and-white. Too often in his accounts the moral struggle becomes a cops-and-robbers story. Too often he lets heroes and villains symbolize the ethical dilemmas of society. But these facts do not defeat the argument that the journalist takes with utmost seriousness his moral responsibility in his community. Indeed, they help to prove it.

Perversions in the Journalist's Role

Sometimes the ethical responsibility of journalism is seen by reversing lenses. You read in your journal that a mother has abandoned her baby. "I had to do it," she is quoted. "The baby is better dead than looking forward to the kind of life I could provide." How does it happen that that story got into the newspapers? Why is it news? In a negative way, the moral truth is affirmed that infanticide is wrong. Suppose you belonged to a culture that found no moral offense in infanticide and a kind of prudent virtue in the explanation that the mother gave. The story would never have made the newspapers. It would have had no moral meaning. All the time, journalism tips its hand in moral matters and reveals what it considers just and good by what it presents as wrong.

Let's be realistic. It is perfectly evident that some organs of journalism overwork their moral indignation when the pursuit of evil is exciting, or the smell is titillating to the nostrils, or the role of avenging angel is self-serving. You can see the power for good or ill in the abuses of that power, and you can become cynical about the moral integrity of institutions that tut-tut indignantly about "Sin Street" during circulation slumps, or use their rapier of justice to knife a private enemy. No one can be happy about these perversions of the journalist's role. He can only hope they are perversions that, in the end, will prove self-defeating rather than self-serving. There are signs that communities know how to lose their respect for the moral integrity of institutions that habitually waste their moral fervor or misdirect it to selfish ends.

Public Morality

The highest goals of journalism are invariably stated in moral terms. To inform the people, to serve the public interest, to combat injustice, to promote the general welfare, to play fair—these infinitives could well serve as a paraphrase of the Canons of Journalism of the American Society of Newspaper Editors or of the statements of purpose off the mastheads of many newspapers. The electronic media are by law required to serve the "public interest, convenience, and necessity," and have gone beyond the law in drafting codes for themselves that pledge their moral purposes even more explicitly. To be sure, this is all canonical writing and is subject to some suspicion for its grandiloquence. Even if the institutions of journalism had spoken more candidly and said their purposes were "to make a buck" or "to sell tooth-paste," they would still have had to gain those ends through public service and moral usefulness to their communities.

If one doubts the moral purpose of journalism, he needs only to observe the reporter on his beat, the anger that flares up in him at injustice, his indignation at the heartlessness of a housing eviction, his disgust at official corruption, his pain at the death of a child in the street. To fight an evil, to expose a wrong, to produce or conserve a social good —you will find few reporters who aren't ahead of you in those crusades.

The highest award in American journalism, the coveted Pulitzer Prize for disinterested and meritorious public service, reflects year after year this preoccupation of the newspaper with concerns affecting public morality. Examine just a few of the exploits of these winners:

The *Arkansas Gazette* of Little Rock confronted the crisis of 1957 in its city, as its Central High School proceeded toward racial integration and, at great cost to itself, led the people toward the restoration of calmness and order. Five years before, two weekly newspapers in North Carolina gained the prize for their campaigns against the Ku Klux Klan in their own towns, campaigns that resulted in the conviction of over 100 Klansmen and an end of terrorism in their communities.

Consider the *Chicago Daily News,* cleaning out a $2,500,000 fraud in the office of the State Auditor of Illinois and sending him and his conspirators to jail. Or the *St. Louis Post-Dispatch,* reforming the mine safety laws after the disasters in the coalfields of southern Illinois, or exposing corruption in the Internal Revenue Bureau, or ridding St. Louis of the smoke nuisance.

Reforming election laws, safeguarding the ballot, exposing conspiracies between law officers and criminal elements,
telling the people of race track scandals and labor racketeer-
ing—these are only a few of the services of newspapers that
have won them Pulitzer Prizes. They demonstrate the role
of journalism as moral conscience of the community.

There is an Episcopal rector in the heart of congested
Manhattan who has become a warrior for justice in housing
practices in New York City. He knows the extent of criminality, the laxity in enforcing the laws, the inadequacy of
the laws, and the resulting hardship to individuals and families. No one would argue that the church does not own its
right to fight this kind of battle. Who has leaped to the
rector's support? All the forces of organized religion, aroused
by his alarm, throwing their massive weight into an effort
to clean up housing malpractice in the city? All the enforce-
ment agencies of the law? All the bureaucrats and officials?
The chief support of James A. Gusweller has come from the
press, from newspaper, magazine, tract and book, from radio
and television, these institutions of journalism that take
seriously their call to moral responsibility in society.

Why Journalism Deals with Holy Things

Look again at some of these basic characteristics of journalism: its capacity for social usefulness; its moral concern;
its devotion to the Word, to record, to utterance; its belief
in human communication; its appreciation of history and its
sensitivity to the crisis in human history; the dedication of
its talents to the pursuit of truth and freedom. Is it too much
to say that these are holy things? That the journalist begins
his function in a house filled with sacramental objects and
holy purposes? He may function badly and defile the temple.

He gains no personal sanctity by the mere fact of inhabiting the house. But he is in a place of vocation, where God calls and where man may respond to the call.

These chapters have been written to show a fundamental religious responsibility upon anyone who goes to work with the values and duties of journalism; indeed, a Christian responsibility. It is not usual to define journalism in just this way. Its highest ideals are frequently stated, and they are almost always in a secular terminology, tidily ethical, having to do with such prudent virtues as honesty, fairness, decency, and public service. The vocation of journalism, however, is more than response to a neat list of professional ethical standards. One who senses the religious dimension of his calling to journalism has insights and instincts that illuminate a much wider field. Falsehood is one thing when viewed as a technical infraction of an internal professional code. It is something else, and more profoundly to be regretted, when viewed as an offense against the family of man and God's purposes for his family. The Christian in journalism is motivated more surely and compelled more urgently than is another who simply places himself at the service of the profession. The sense of stewardship of one's talents, the sense of vocation, is a curious thing. Nothing much may appear to the naked eye. The total effectiveness of one who has given himself in faithful response to God's plan may not add up to anything greater (and may appear less) than the effectiveness of the accidental achiever who leaves indelible marks upon his life and times. The walk along the road of one's lifework to the eventual, "Well done, thou good and faithful servant," is, after all, a walk alone with God, and only He and the walker know the measurable statistics of the travel.

Stressing the religious dimensions of the journalistic calling, as has been done here, may raise painful questions among those present. Secular journalists may protest that they wish no sanctification of their purposes and will reject as "labored" the paragraphs that have been written here to give sacred responsibilities to their craft. Others, who know the history of journalism and the rich contributions that have been made to it by devoted Jews, or humanists, or pagans, or other religiously oriented faithful, will resent the Christian label on this discourse. Certain professional Christians, whose clericalism is probably better than their religion, will find these ideas somewhat profane and so much justification of the secular, cultural *status quo.*

The "religious journalist" (quoted) is a convenient manufacture for both the church and the journalistic world. He is the man who writes a serious call to a devout and holy life, or covers sermons for the Monday Times, or edits a mimeographed newssheet for the southernmost parish of the Old North Church. He is the technical specialist within the profession. Or, he is the writer who separates himself from the mainstream of human communication to bear his witness in a special place. These are certainly religious journalists, without any quotation marks.

But, meanwhile, there are those who cover fires, or police courts, or the parliaments of man. These, too, have a religious claim upon them, for they are involved in communicating human intelligence, in exchanging those most precious things, the thoughts of men and the raw data of human experience that feed the mind and soul and lead to thoughtful, responsible membership in the human family.

God has lordship over all of life. He meets his servants not only at the altar, not only in isolated moments of private

communication, not only in ritualistic and legalistic ad-
herence to certain approved behavioral works, not only in
the ecstatic response of prophets and saints. He meets them
everywhere. The New Testament, and the Reformation
revival of it, had much to say about the stewardship of a
multiplicity of talents and gifts, all of which could be used
in faithful response to the Lord of life. One's daily work
gains significance because right there, within the particular
necessities and forms of that daily work, the decisions that
must be made and the purposes that must be served, one
may find his way to a Christian ministry.

CHAPTER THREE

The Ambiguous Base ... Freedom

If you take seriously your sense of vocation in journalism, and wish to use it and its institutions as the arena for the stewardship of your talents, you will develop a marked sensitivity to a host of problems that confront you and your colleagues in the field. The problems may loom larger, and disturb you more profoundly, precisely because you have taken on a kind of ministry in this field. Hopefully, you may be able to bring light and understanding and solution to some of them, precisely because you have a vocation that gives you a broader stance from which to judge them.

Problems of a Free Press

It is time to look at these problems. Some of them have to do with the basic philosophies and ideologies that flow through the journalism you will serve. Some are institutional, some methodological, some personal. One of the first that will confront you affects the very foundations of journalism and its institutions. This is the problem of the freedom of the press.

Your first impulse will be to think that press freedom is hardly a debatable issue. It was settled in 1789 when the constitutional protections of the free press were written into the First Amendment. The truth is that press freedom is a continuing issue, both within the United States and without, and not all the enemies of that freedom are deep-dyed villains. You might even be one of them.

Society is without question given the right to protect itself. It can pass laws to regulate property—common, corporate, and private. It can legislate and enforce its laws to protect the lives of its people. It can require that the food that goes into the mouths of its people shall not poison them. It can require that drugs and medicine do not damage the health of their users. Does it seem strange that the law can do nothing to affect what goes into the minds of its people?

Dare a society run the risk of a half-informed people, or a wrongly informed people, or an overinformed people? Does it not have the right to inform the people concerning the way it wishes to preserve order internally and security from without? Social stability is a worthy value, too. Why should the freedom of a "blabbermouth" press take precedence over that value? And since the instruments of social stability are and must be in the hands of the government, should not the government have some rights of its own over against the rights of the press?

A United States airplane is attacked by Soviet fighters. Moscow says it was on aerial reconnaissance within the borders of the Soviet Union. Washington says it was far away measuring cosmic rays. The conflict may be of world-shattering consequence. Is it so important, in the face of this threat to the whole world society, that the public know the truth? Who cares?

A highly technical line-budget has been prepared by elected officials after months of study and deliberation and the advice of experts. It is presented to the people, whose taxes will pay the bills. The people question and quibble. They have had no expert advice, have made no study, do not know the reasons that have brought every line in that budget into being. To handle the intricacies of a modern, technical budget aren't the people really incompetent? Why should the democratic dream of a free, informed public be permitted to become a nightmare of confusion and inefficiency? Why should everybody in town know the salary of every teacher in the school system? What do the people know about measuring the trajectory of one missile over another?

A press photographer catches the distortions of grief on the face of a mother who has just seen the drowned body of her child on the beach. A newspaper prints columns of purple prose snatched from the private diary of a sick personality. A reporter invades the secrecy of the jury room. The personal, private troubles of two persons become public property as they are aired in the divorce court. Reports of crime breed more crime. Waves of juvenile delinquency are invented by the press. Passions are inflamed by the press in racial conflicts, in international tensions, in labor-management differences. One party to an argument can get his case stated in the newspapers or on the air; the other can't be heard. Is there no power on earth to control and curb these offenses, these excesses?

The First Amendment and the American tradition of a free press are rooted in the libertarian philosophies of western Europe that arose to oppose the tyrannies of a dying order no longer expressive of the vitalities of the times. Vigorous, new revolutionary forces were at work in the society, and the resulting new explosion of thought could not be held in check by muzzling the voices, licensing the vehicles of print, by censorship and punishment. The mood of free inquiry was dominant in philosophy, education, religion, in the new science and invention, and in politics and statecraft.

The Power of Truth

If every man in every walk freely pursued the truth, and if no authority were permitted to intervene in or deflect this pursuit, he would approach the truth, expose the false, and all his institutions and establishments would be sound, and true, and just, by virtue of the integrity built into them. The liberal education, the march of science, the reform of the church, the democratic state—all these establishments gained impetus. The whole theory of libertarianism fell apart if any sand got into the wheels of man's progress toward the truth. That sand was authority, whether by state or crown or church or disproved tradition. The pursuit of truth became divine right, and no longer could the church or crown lay claim to it.

> And though all the winds of doctrine were let loose to play upon the earth, so Truth be in the field, we do injuriously by licensing and prohibiting to misdoubt her strength. Let her and Falsehood grapple; who ever knew Truth put to the worse, in a free and open encounter? ... For who knows not that Truth is strong,

next to the Almighty? She needs no policies, no strata-
gems, no licensings to make her victorious; those are the
shifts and the defenses that error uses against her power.
Give her but room, and do not bind her. . . . [1]

Thus John Milton wrote in words that have rung down
through the age of democracy like trumpet sounds. Jefferson knew them, and echoed them in many of his own writings. Tom Paine knew them. The charters of American
democracy are imbued with the spirit of Milton and others
like him. Furthermore, working within this philosophical
mood was a cocky, militant, aggressive press, and restrictive
acts of the antidemocrats—there were some—gave way before its militancy. The press does not get its right to freedom from the state or any other awarding authority. The
people have a divine right to pursue the truth freely. This
comes first. State and authority come later as instruments
that a free people have set up freely to serve their free pursuit of truth. Here is the reason that Congress "shall make
no law . . . abridging the freedom of speech or of the press."
Here is the reason that to this day the American press shoul-
ders a responsibility of freedom unlike that of any other
nation of the world. Here is the reason American representatives stand so stubbornly alone in international gatherings
and in the United Nations Sub-Commission on Freedom of
Information and the Press. Other nations, less certain than
Milton about the triumph of truth in the market place of
ideas, more realistic about power and its uses, less secure
in their own power, more jealous and intolerant in their
own anointed roles, feel that order is too much to risk to
the disharmonious assault of a free press, or even free
public inquiry.

Freedom—a Paradoxical Thing

A person who comes into journalism with some sense of history, and particularly with some sense of Christian history, will never be quite so absolutist as were Milton and company about freedom. It is a paradoxical thing. There is a line in a Christian hymn of George Matheson, "Make me a captive, Lord, and then I shall be free." This expresses the paradox of absolute freedom. Freedom is relative and is a condition of other, more absolute ideas. For historical reasons, the libertarians of the seventeenth century were concerned for freedom *from* the powers and elements that restrained their restless vitalities. Once the restraints were contained, the emphasis shifted to a concern for freedom *to* get on with the job. This emphasis brings difficulties. It is as if history were saying, "All right, you've got your freedom now. What are you going to do with it?"

Certainly there have been abuses of freedom of the press. Milton and the author of the First Amendment were slightly naïve, optimistic, and unrealistic. Law in the United States has known this, and has gone quite a distance in abridging the freedoms that the Constitution wrote about. For instance, the press can not maliciously defame a person without risking severe penalties under the law. You will be expected to learn the intricacies of the laws of libel and defamation, and the defenses against them, when you begin to bear your responsibilities in journalism. It will do you no good to stand dogmatically on your belief that the press is free and above the law when you are being sued for $200,000 in a civil court because of something defamatory you have authored in the free press.

Certain critics of the press point out that no institution

in America stands so sublimely beyond control as does the press. It can be an evil, antisocial instrument, they argue, and no power on earth can do anything about it. Actually, this is not quite true. In the first place, the church probably stands farther off from the eye of the law than does the newspaper. In the second, the press is haltered by a long list of limitations on its freedom, and is continually engaged in struggles to redefine those limitations. Press freedom is not nearly so absolute as many of its critics claim.

Necessary Curbs on Freedom

Though it is not so likely to happen in this country as it would be in England, you can be cited for contempt by the law for any publication of yours that interferes with the course of justice. You can observe a case at law, and report it, but you are not a member of the jury, nor the judge. If you start to usurp those roles, you run the risk of citation for contempt.

By a curious necessity in a technological age, the press is subject to licensing by the state. This may seem hard to believe among a people whose first newspaper, Boston's *Publick Occurrences*, defied licensing by the Governor and was banned after one issue, a people who found part of their soul in resistance to the Stamp Act. But it is true. The electronic media of communications can't begin to operate without licenses from the Federal Communications Commission, a regulatory agency of the federal government. To be sure, there are mechanical, technical reasons for this situation. There are only so many frequencies, and some authority must be responsible for allocating them. In exchange for a license, a broadcaster pledges himself to serve "the public interest, convenience, and necessity." Theoretically at least, if he fails to serve that interest, his license can be taken away. One should take note of ways that this licensing power, which began as a technical necessity, can be stretched to cover the substance of broadcasting. Fraudulent show business, payola, the quiz scandals can be controlled through the license. It can be invoked to insure equal-time practices on the air, whereby all voices and all opinions have the same opportunities to be heard. These may seem to be reasonable assertions of power, but, once the power is there, when might it be used capriciously, punitively to enforce a whim (or even a conviction) of the FCC?

All governments with some regard for libertarian principles have known the dilemma of freedom when it challenges the governments themselves. Obviously, freedom has to be restrained when it comes to the point of wrecking the society. The issue of sedition, subversion, revolution, hostile thoughts has been an issue that government has used its power to meet. Sometimes successfully, sometimes unsuccessfully. This power, however used, is another restraint upon absolute freedom of the press.

The United States government has used seizure, censorship, criminal penalties to curb the freedom of speech and of the press when it felt the steps were necessary. One recalls with no great feeling of pride the days of the Alien and Sedition Acts. Lincoln briefly locked the doors of certain Copperhead newspapers during the Civil War. There has been censorship, as one would have to expect, in all the nation's wars. Fortunately, the practices of censorship have become more adult as the nation has matured, and have come to be based on codes of mutual consent between gov-

ernment and press with a minimum of restraint and a max-
imum of freedom. The only exception to this statement is
the government's use of censorship through the post office.
It has become increasingly juvenile through the years. Di-
rected toward control of the distribution of obscene matter,
this censorship strives to protect the public from base por-
nography, a legitimate objective, but succeeds mostly in
stifling expression and adding fuel to the pornographic fire.

The government has other tricks of control in its bag. It
requires publishers of material traceable to foreign ideologies to register themselves and declare their authorship.
(Happily, this ordinance has never been applied against the
publications of the Christian church or the followers of
John Locke.) It can tax. It can control imports from abroad,
such things as newsprint and foreign documents. It can
regulate the legal corporations that are the institutional
bodies of the press, and has done so in the cases of the
Associated Press and the *Kansas City Star*. The entire newspaper industry is, in fact, regulated by the Fair Labor
Standards Act and the National Labor Relations Act, among
other regulatory measures that govern United States corporations.

"A Clear and Present Danger"

The best wisdom that has been brought to bear upon this
dilemma of how far the law should go in restraining sedition is summed up in the "clear and present danger" test
of Justice Holmes. "The question in every case is whether
the words used are used in such circumstances and are of
such a nature as to create a clear and present danger that
they will bring about the substantive evils that Congress

has a right to prevent," he wrote in the decision on Schenck *vs.* United States in 1919. All government has a duty to preserve order within its borders. If it can be shown that utterance or publication creates a clear and present danger to that order, the law may be used to restrain and to punish. The circumstances make a difference. A drillmaster on a rifle range who shouts, "Fire!" is obviously in a different situation from that of a mad man in a theater who screams the same word. The nature of the utterance or publication makes a difference. Inflammatory material openly inciting to violence, riot, and rebellion, is different from the poetry of Walt Whitman.

A fanatical Nazi orator requests a permit to speak in New York's Union Square in the spring of 1960, and is refused. Was there a clear and present danger? Or did the law go farther than it should have gone? Another fanatic distributes handbills urging resistance to the military draft in time of war. Was there a clear and present danger? The law must find the subtle answer to this question as it weighs the concerns for public order over against the people's claim to freedom.

A Cause of International Disagreements

It is precisely this issue that has caused the United States so much trouble in international conversations on press freedom. American doctrine and practice permit of much more freedom than other countries are willing to concede. Judicial decisions here tend to put government on the defensive, to assume the freedom right as a basic condition and to allow governmental restraint only in extreme cases. Other countries, even those with sound democratic traditions, tend to put the shoe on the other foot: to assume the government's right to protect itself and to make the critic defend his right to criticize. This is the issue that has made impossible any agreement in the U. N. Sub-Commission on Freedom of Information and the Press. For example, an editor in a foreign capital writes a piece critical of the head of state. He is accused of disturbing the peace on grounds reminiscent of the medieval offense of *lèse-majesté,* of weakening his country before the world, of irresponsible use of his freedom for seditious purposes. He is jailed, and American editors look on in horror. The ink is not yet dry on their latest blast against the American chief of state, and no one thinks for a moment that the foundations of the Republic are threatened. The press of the world has not been able to synthesize these two points of view.

Because of the scope of citizens' liberty in this country, and because the courts tend to decide as they do, another device of governmental restraint has been developing here that is currently the cause of considerable worry and fury among press and public alike. It is the tendency of government, of the bureaucrats, of the "ins," to avoid criticism by hiding. Not doing public business in public is a growing practice. Issuing publicity handouts, making press statements, classifying much government business as secret, freezing the news at the source—these are the means that this type of control applies. Since the newspapers opened the proceedings of Parliament to the public in the late 1700's, the victory for openness in democratic government had been considered won. Not so. Actions in the Pentagon and in the smallest town council meeting of the land are done behind closed doors, out of the sight of public and press.

A Press Too Free?

Is the press too free? Do you really worry about this uncontrolled giant, accountable to no one? Many people do. This was the chief worry of the most serious study made of the press in recent years, that of the so-called Hutchins commission, the Commission on the Freedom of the Press. Many persons think that it came close to suggesting that government should get back into the act of controlling the media of communications, not to make the nation safe for tyranny, but to save the people from the tyranny of irresponsible newspapers, magazines, radio, television, movies. The Commission did not invite government control. Indeed, most of its suggestions gained urgency as measures that should be taken to forestall government control. It suggested self-criticism within the press, boards of review, freer competition, and a competition of ideas among the media, as well as criticism and review by educational institutions.

The idea of a board of review is a persistent one, some kind of quasi-official but nongovernmental panel of public spirits that will keep the press under scrutiny and air its criticisms when it spots misbehavior. Every sober study of the press is certain to produce at least one voice that calls for the establishment of some kind of board of review. The idea keeps its currency partly on its own merits, but mostly because of the practice in Britain where public bodies, and even Parliament, do strive to keep the press under surveillance and publicize their criticisms. Anyone in Britain who feels that he has a just complaint against the press can take it to the General Council of the Press. This body will then investigate and report its findings. A school that objects to press photographers' invading its premises, a professional society that feels its standards have been maligned, an amateur swimming team that was inaccurately reported as competing for pay—none of these cases is damaging enough to justify legal action, perhaps, but is the kind of complaint that may be publicly aired by taking it to the General Council. When, in the autumn of 1960, the liberal *News-Chronicle* in London was sold to a large British newspaper chain, and disappeared, again the outcry for a public inquiry took up. What were the circumstances surrounding the disappearance of the daily? Was justice done to the employees who lost their jobs? Was there a danger to democracy through the growing concentration of newspaper ownership in a few hands? Even the House of Commons, when it convened, took up these questions in its debates and acted as a public board of review scrutinizing the behavior of the press. Many persons feel that these British examples have meaning for the American scene, and that American journalism needs the watchful eye of a body with power to investigate and criticize what the press does with its freedom.

Some of this same concern has been shared by Sigma Delta Chi, honorary journalistic fraternity. It investigated the possibility of setting up a public board of review that would play watchdog on the press during a recent presidential campaign year. It would check the media on their ways of handling the campaign news, on their fairness in the news columns, on their contributions to healthy public debate, on their coloration and slanting of the news in favor of their preferred candidates. Nothing came of this effort, although it was ready to roll. The fact that a responsible

fraternity within a profession feels the need of such an
effort in critical moments in the nation's history shows again
the concern in high places that something should be done
to enforce public responsibility on the press.

For some persons within the profession, such proposals
as these raise more questions than they answer. For one
thing, the reintroduction of the idea of government control
(any more than there is) offends most of this country's
basic philosophic and constitutional beliefs. Government is
the easiest locus of control, because it has power. But the
assumption that the government's interest is identical with
the people's interest is exactly the false assumption that the
Tory governors made against the infant American press and
that all governments will always make. For another, there
is an unresolved confusion in these proposals about the
role of the press. Is it a public utility merely, feeding a
minimal diet of sanitary groceries into the public's innocent mouths? Or is it expected to be opinionated, even
at the risk of error, assertive of some leadership, reflective
of some personality? Is there not something patronizing in
the attitude that the public must be protected from the
Henry Luces, the Colonel McCormicks, the Harry Goldens,
the Tom Paines? Is it impossible for the public to discrim-
inate and protect itself? Granted, it is not easy to answer
these questions categorically. But it is true that a press that
is too canon-bound never to offend the public interest can
become conformist, bland, and ineffectual, just as a press
that is too personal, pamphleteering, and opinionated can
become flagrant, disruptive, and antisocial.

Possible Controls over Excessive Freedom

The problem remains of the conditions and centers of control over this enormous institution of mass communication within society. Government will play its part, and the part should not be enlarged by much. Another locus of control is the public itself. A publisher will frequently say with some arrogance that no one needs to worry about enforcing social responsibility on him. "I am under daily control by the little man with the nickel (or 7 cents or a dime) in his pocket." There is something to this remark. One can find evidence of newspapers, other journals, and other media that lose their public support by abusing the public interest, by tasteless sensationalism, and by too extreme opinions. One can also find immensely valuable properties that earn their way with a good product.

There could be much more control of the mass media through mutual criticism. For some timid reason a gentlemen's agreement seems to exist among competing media that they must never talk about each other. A few breakthroughs have been registered against this gentlemen's agreement. The longest, strongest tradition in press criticism, starting with Will Irwin's series on the American newspaper in *The American* in 1911, has been the critique by magazines of the other media. Radio and television have occasionally programed reviews and critiques of the press. Some newspapers will debate openly with other newspapers, and more should express themselves in controversy and dialogue when opinions and emphases differ. There should be no "professional ethics" that hides open discussion under a cloak of courtesy. It is no courtesy to the public interest to bring silence into the fields where ideas play.

Schools of journalism and professional societies should engage themselves in continuing criticism, review, study, and research that bring the media under constant judgment. Already a great deal of control has been asserted upon the media from these centers and has resulted in professional improvements, raising of standards, lessening of irresponsibility.

The ultimate control upon the press is from the inside out. Codes and canons are only partial steps toward the kind of self-discipline that should be in such firm control that responsible behavior is automatic. In the 1956 campaign for the presidency a prominent group of newspapers took upon itself a practice of giving equal play in the news columns to the chief contenders. In matched columns, with equivalent space, similar headlines, and comparable photographic treatment these newspapers let the facts of the campaign speak for themselves. On the editorial pages of the same newspapers they made their preferences known and debated the issues, but no preferential treatment was allowed to leak into the news presentment. This whole practice was a responsibility assumed by the newspapers themselves.

Responsibility—a Precondition of Freedom

Would it have been preferable to have the procedure imposed from without? By government, by a board of review, by a court of censors? Certainly not. All observers of the American press will tell you that the most marked change in journalistic history in this country in recent years has been in the direction of self-discipline in responsibility. Journalistic spokesmen are not so inclined as they once were to speak in hallowed tones of the "free press," but of the "free and responsible press." The slogan is more than words only; you can see the differences in actual press practice from city to city in the country. The stress upon responsibility is a whole new factor introduced into the formula of journalistic practice, and it alters the basic definition of the profession. One can still see abuses of the freedom of the press, immaturity, and distorted views of the public interest. But, in perspective, the changes in the direction of social responsibility on the part of the press are apparent. One would misread history if he were not to note these changes. The Christian in journalism should never hesitate in moments of decision making to insist upon responsibility as a precondition of freedom. Indeed, he probably more than others should have understood freedom's ambiguities. He should have known from the depths of his belief that freedom becomes a viable social good when it is in bondage to the truth and to responsibility.

In a recent speech at the University of Michigan, Robert Estabrook, editor of the editorial page of the *Washington Post and Times-Herald,* spent an hour detailing in penetrating analysis the shortcomings of the press. Nevertheless, he summed up his remarks by saying, "I think that we have a basically responsible press today. I think that it has shown many broad improvements in method and content over the last fifty years."

Don't look so far for the big-brotherly hand to be raised to enforce social responsibility upon the press. Wash your own. Improvements and growth in responsibility have come about in the press largely upon the initiative of the men and women in it. Their competence, their skills, their social concerns, their ideals and purposes have produced whatever improvement there is. If you, as you enter the profession,

are concerned for better standards, more responsible behavior, some measure of discipline and control against irresponsible, shoddy practice, then consider the kind of standards, skills, and self-control that you contribute. The press
is not too free if it is free and responsible.

CHAPTER FOUR

In the System ... Questions

You will encounter another complex of problems in journalism in relation to the institutions through which you do your work. Actually, they are not such bad institutions as institutions go, but you will feel sure at times that you can't fight the bosses and that they are dedicated to the frustration of your purposes and the obliteration of your creative genius. It may be the charming little story you have picked up at the cat show, a delicate little divertissement, and you have it almost all written in feline dialect. The city editor is up to his neck in a city transit strike, and you can't get a purr out of him. Just as you thought, they are out to get you.

But the problem should not be burlesqued. Serious charges have been leveled against the institutions of journalism. You will hear them. You have heard them. And you have some sympathy for them. There is no closed season on shooting at publishers, presidents, and vice presidents. The bookshelf is long that houses the literature muckraking the institutions and overlords of journalism, and you can't get out of college without dipping into that literature. Even novels have taken up the theme. One remembers the movie, "Citizen Kane," and reflects soberly upon the image of the man who swaggers imperiously and brutally through those frames.

A Merchant-Minded Press

The press is owned by business men. It reflects the interests of the merchant class. Aristocratic or intellectual tastes are not its first tastes, nor does it instinctively speak with the inflections of the farmer or worker. It is extraordinarily sensitive to economic pressures and reacts swiftly to economic necessity. It lives intimately with other business men whose wares are advertised in its pages. It is primarily dependent upon advertising for its revenue. It is conservative in almost all things, politics particularly, and resistant to social change.

These charges are not far from the truth. Indeed, they are scarcely charges at all, but simple descriptions of the facts of the situation. Implied in the descriptions, however, are accusations that such a pro-business orientation perverts the purposes of the press as informer of the people, leader of opinion, and critic of the culture. One should seriously examine these accusations and determine to what extent they are true.

Given a merchant-minded press, what are the problems involved? For one thing, its pro-business bias could cloud its reportorial eye toward other social and economic classes and render them voiceless in the public debate. Minority voices might find little or no expression in such a press.

Voices in opposition to business's preferred interests could be denied a chance to speak. For example, it is no secret that the American press was predominantly hostile to the ideas of Franklin D. Roosevelt. Was he silenced in its pages? As he is reported to have said at one time, the editors and publishers had their editorial pages, but he had the front page.

A realistic test of the extent to which the information stream is polluted by the bias of the American press can be made in connection with the voice of labor. Insofar as the press represents the interests of big business, management, the owners, and the merchants, one should expect to find a basic lack of sympathy for the interests of labor. A good many unionists would maintain that they can't be heard in the market place of ideas, and there is a labor press that partially compensates for the space that is denied them in the mass media. The interests of labor are today presented with considerable cogency, and its ideology is open for public debate. Part of the credit for this open situation is labor's, of course—through its own press and radio, its own vocality, its political presence. But part of the credit must also go to the very merchant-minded institutions that one would expect to find closed to the interests of labor. The rise of labor reporting in the mass media in the past thirty years is one of the most striking developments in journalism.

Dependence on Advertisers

The press's chumminess with advertisers and dependence upon them for revenue have led to another set of serious accusations that advertisers determine the editorial content of newspapers and other media and that they sit in the critical spot controlling the flow of information. Everyone has a story or two to prove that advertisers control what goes into the newspapers or over the air. The usual one is the story about the elevator that fell in the department store of the city's biggest advertiser, and no word of the dreadful accident appeared anywhere. Most of these stories could be matched with equally good ones that prove the opposite. A small newspaper prints in its news columns a story offensive to the local bank, the bank withdraws its advertising and tries with some success to enlarge the boycott among merchants along Main Street. Did the newspaper cave in? It did not. It fought and won, and the bank had a serious public relations problem on its hands for years. When the *Arkansas Gazette* took its strong editorial stand for order and fair play during Little Rock's school integration crisis of 1957 it suffered serious financial damage from the withdrawal of support by advertisers who did not share the *Gazette*'s position. Pressure from advertisers determines editorial content? Apparently not in the case of the *Arkansas Gazette*.

But If There Were No Advertisers?

But put the stories aside. The truth is that advertising supports the press. That's the system. The question is whether or not another system would be better, more socially responsible. Suppose the whole burden of supporting the press were placed upon subscribers. This would be the end of the people's press. It would become a class instrument immeasurably more narrowly aimed than it is today. Only the wealthy could afford to buy access to the flow of information. Circulations would shrink. A weaker press would result, one more susceptible to pressures and less independent. Suppose the government picked up the tab for the nation's press. You might get a fairly responsible product, secure and orderly and benevolent, but it would certainly be the end of the American press as it has developed over two centuries. The press as the fourth estate, making its contribution to the body politic by serving as the people's eyes in the halls of government, would be ended. The door would be open to authoritarian journalism. Suppose any other systems of support that you can think of—an endowed press, a foundation-supported press, a party-supported press, a group-supported press. There are examples of these kinds of journalism that you can study in history and observe around you. None of them produces a more vital, independent, and socially responsible press than the system of support from advertising has developed.

Furthermore, one of the social responsibilities of the press, by anybody's definition, would be to support and contribute to the people's common life. A good part of that common life is the people's economy. All civilizations have had their systems of exchange, the oriental bazaar, the market, transport and roads, currencies. Advertising in the press plays a critical economic role. In a sense, it is the medieval market where traders meet and the wheels of commerce are lubricated. The housewife more eagerly awaits the Thursday afternoon supermarket advertisement in her newspaper than she awaits the news on the front page. If all the ads in the newspaper were removed, there would still have to be space devoted to the prices of products and the places where they are available, because these matters are news of critical importance in any community.

You will still continue to be suspicious of this power that lurks behind the business offices of the press. And you should. You will read a column of news that seems in-

ordinately kind to a certain manufacturer or product, and
you will note his ad in an adjoining column. You will become weary of the leggy photographs of the lovelies who
have just arrived by courtesy of Skybound Airways. You
will see and regret that many newspapers no longer mention
books, review them or report the news of them, and you
will realize that books don't advertise. You will hear that
conspiracies along Madison Avenue, where the advertising
agencies are supposed to dwell, can chill and kill a magazine. You will be told about "business office musts"—stories
that must be written and printed by orders of the powers
in the countinghouse. You will be thoroughly disgusted by
sponsors' control over program content on radio and television, and deeply worried about the freedom of the arts
and the press when advertisers hold it in such total control.

But you will also learn some other things after your initia-
tion into journalism. You will learn that institutions that
truckle to their advertisers lose their own self-respect, the
trust of the community, and the respect of the advertisers
themselves. You will learn that direct pressure upon editorial
content from an advertiser is infrequent, and when it comes
it is so subtle and devious that it is a manageable editorial
problem. You will find that the support of the press is advertising, but not advertisers. The more sound is the economic base of an institution and the more wide and diverse
its advertising revenues, the more able is that institution
to tell an individual coercive and abusive advertiser to go
jump in the Jumna. What's more, he generally comes back.

You will have other doubts about these business-based
houses of journalism. One of your deepest worries will concern the fact that as the literate population increases, as circulations go up and the institutions of journalism become

stronger, they also become fewer. Probably the saddest days in journalism—and they have been altogether too numerous —are the days that the closing notices go up on bulletin boards across the land. Your friends are out of work, and another voice in journalism has been stilled. Mergers, consolidations, sales. There is no mistaking this trend. There are fewer journalistic houses today than there were. Fifty years ago well more than half of American cities had competing daily newspapers. Today, only one out of every twenty cities has more than one newspaper ownership. Twenty states have no cities with daily newspaper competition. In Cleveland, Pittsburgh, San Francisco, Columbus— one by one they go. Did Hearst have nothing more to say in Pittsburgh, in Chicago? No public duty, no roots, no loyalty? It was just a business, and when the property failed to show the expected profit it had to go.

"We who are in newspaper work might as well face the fact that we are in a contracting business," the publisher of the Louisville newspapers told the class of 1960 at the Columbia Graduate School of Journalism, "not as to circulation perhaps, but as to the number of newspapers, the number of people employed on them and the number of newspaper proprietors."

Monopoly Ownership—a Potential Danger

Monopoly ownership of the outlets for the dissemination of information in this country is a problem worrying more people than you. The growth of group newspapers or chain ownership is rapid and picking up speed. One hundred and ten chains control more than half the circulation of United States dailies. There are now only two news agencies in this country providing wire copy to their subscribers and members; only a few years ago there were three. Many newspapers own the radio and television outlets in their cities, a situation that tightens the monopoly. In some cities competing newspapers are merging their facilities and producing from the same plant. Some journalistic corporations are today producers of newspapers, books, and magazines as well as being owners of radio-television stations.

It is not hard to see the potential danger. Where is the market place of ideas if only one voice can be heard? What becomes of the free press, which was a guarantee that the people could speak, could inform themselves, could inquire and debate, if the free press itself by the logic of its own economics becomes monolithic and total? No one should underestimate this danger.

The Safeguard of Other Competitive Media

There are some considerations, however, that should be set alongside your worries about the trend toward monopolization in American journalism. The peril of monopoly would be the stilling of debate and the controlling of the information stream. Press monopoly has grown precisely at a time when information never moved more swiftly and the people have debated and made some of the most critical decisions of their history. In practice, the danger has not been realized. Speed and efficiency of communication have increased so phenomenally that they have overcome any restraining effect that monopoly might have desired. Radio and television, special publications, word of mouth, the host of informal newsletters that have appeared—it would be difficult for a newspaper to try to monopolize the conversation against all these competitors in the public forum. Also, it would be fair to say that the monopoly newspapers have not tried to use their positions restrictively. In almost all cases the monopoly newspapers are fairer, more socially responsible and sounder institutions than the competing newspapers they replaced. Though competition frequently leads to efforts to outsensationalize the rest of the field, noncompetitive newspapers can afford to proceed with more balance, perspective, and taste. For example: imagine a city in which there are two competing dailies, one a sharp-tongued Democratic sheet, the other Republican. The Democratic bias becomes more pronounced in the Democratic paper, the Republican bias in the other. In the economy of journalism in that city, one paper has to be content with approximately half of everything, income, circulation, advertising, influence. Remove one paper, and the resulting institution is suddenly in possession of everything. The Democratic sheet may not lose its editorial punch, but it knows that half its readers belong to the other party, and their interests merit some attention in the paper. The monopoly newspaper tends to become less partisan and more a public institution. The monopoly newspaper tends to be stronger and more independent than competing newspapers whose weak points make them susceptible to pressures and disease that stronger institutions can withstand. The monopoly newspaper tends to be more objective in handling the news, less strident, less inclined to manufacture stories, more thorough and comprehensive.

One more thing about the monopoly newspaper. Sometimes it is a brand-new paper in a mushrooming town and, thus, is an added voice in the communications network. Some of these new papers are producing with radically new equipment and technical procedures. Big and expensive presses have been replaced with inexpensive offset models. The traditional composing room, where few basic changes have been made since Gutenberg, has been bypassed; and cameras, chemicals, and typewriters have taken the place of lead-casting procedures. Technical innovations in printing may reverse the trend toward monopoly, as more entrepreneurs with less capital can afford to get into the economics of publishing.

While we are on the subject of the institutions of journalism, we need to consider some very practical and personal matters. A few pages ago Mark Ethridge was quoted as saying that journalism was a contracting business, with fewer institutions, fewer persons employed. Where does that leave you? Many discouraging things have been spoken about careers in journalism, and you can't be blamed for questioning the prospect of attaching yourself and your talent to a withering plant. Mr. Ethridge is probably right that the newspaper itself is a tightening market for your talents. Nevertheless, there are still many places for you on the newspapers of the land, and most editors bewail the scarcity of recruits as they scour the offices and colleges for needed men. The communications industry is still one of the most vital in the economy, and growing more vigorous every day. You need to realize the scope and diversification of it. When Ben Franklin "went into journalism," he meant very clearly that he entered the employ of the *New England Courant,* a newspaper. Today, going into journalism can mean a thousand things. Interestingly enough, in almost all its branches it continues to show a strong preference for persons trained on newspapers. So the base of the industry has not changed completely.

There is the journalism of the air, two growing media that may be on the threshold of much more vigorous and exciting experiences in news and public affairs. There is the journalism of the special interests, a flourishing field. You can hardly conceive of the hundreds of publications that prosper by serving the interests of stamp collectors, Presbyterians, children, flower growers, bond dealers, and all the other hobbyists and specialists who make up the myriad groupings of American life. There is, of course, the thriving journalism of American corporations. They, too, have words they want to say to their employees, their owners, their customers, their friends, their neighbors, and though the communicative purpose is self-serving and limited in its pursuit of truth, the skills of the journalist are required to give form to this purpose. Public relations is a journalistic field, giving a communicative voice to industry, to government, to the Amercan Cancer Society, to the local hospital or library. Advertising is not unrelated. There are the magazines, the newsletters, trade journalism. If you add up all the journalistic opportunities, you will not be so alarmed by Mr. Ethridge's words.

Journalism—a Paying Job

And now a little parenthetical secret. The institutions of journalism pay you for your talent. Money. If this bothers you or seems slightly profane, jump along and read ahead. They pay money. Not enough, but it's getting better. The American Newspaper Guild, which is the trade union of editorial workers on newspapers, has firmed the base of newspaper pay; and, though figures vary, you can look forward to from $75 to $100 a week to begin, from $125 to $175 a week when you've completed your apprenticeship. These are minimums. They are low, and the industry is wrong for its stubborn tendency to treat minimums as maximums. A few newspapers are breaking out and rewarding superior talent with superior pay. Salaries of $10,000 a year are becoming more common on newspapers, and there are raises as you take on more responsibilities that will keep you up with most of the other Joneses on your street. Newspapers have been too happy to pay you in psychic income, with your freedom, with by-lines, with the prestige of your position ("he's a reporter for the Bugle!"), and with no objection if you write a novel and sell it to the movies for a fortune. (Not all books are sold to the movies!)

These psychic incomes are real, but newspapers should not be excused for substituting them for the green stuff that buys beets. Most other branches of journalism have a higher base of pay. The electronic media pay about 50 per cent more for comparable work than do newspapers. Salaries in some positions in industrial journalism, public relations, and on some magazines are so fat that the federal tax collectors have an insatiable curiosity about them. The real truth about recompense in any field is that the statistical average is not necessarily you. Just because $8\frac{1}{2}$ is the average size of the male foot, that will not make the average shoe fit your size 12 any more comfortably. Some clergymen make more money than some doctors. You might be surprised at the ranges of income among lawyers, a profession customarily regarded as highly paid. Your colleague who goes out on commencement day to $125 in industrial public relations, while you sign on for $79.37 (take-home) with the Bungleton Blatt, may be counting $137.50 each week after you have hit $175. End of the parenthesis.

Situations That Will Trouble You

Part of the reason that you are in the houses of journalism is responsible for the discomfort that you have in being there. Your worries about business-minded publishers, about the economics of journalism, about pressure from advertisers, about monopolistic tendencies, about institutional conservatism stem from a quality in you that brought you to journalism in the first place. You have not much regard for (and perhaps a fear of) the organization man. Although so much of American economic life has become incorporated, depersonalized, and highly organized, you chose journalism because you felt that you saved a little piece of personality in that choice, that journalism for you was the field in which you could be more immediately effective with your personal talents and ideals. The freedom was attractive. You would not be confined in any corporation jail, and you would keep your individuality from being submerged, fused, and lost in the monster organization.

Now you find that journalism is housed in institutions, after all. And you worry about fitting yourself into your organization. You will be required to conform to policies that seem offensive to your conscience. Take, for example, the matter of where your journal is aimed, the level of its audience. You feel that another man's mind should be respected, that you don't overestimate his information, but you must never underestimate his intelligence. You believe that you should communicate with him cleanly, literately, paying respect to human reason and language. Yet, by direction, you seem to be vulgarizing all subject matter and form. This is the paper's policy, its level, its aim. It will seem that you are required to write only words of five letters and sentences of twelve words. Someone made a read-ability study, and the order came down from on high, and you are convinced that you are tied to a conspiracy to de-grade all mentality and language. Many policies will dis-turb you. Your newspaper refuses to take a stand in the presence of a situation you are certain is unjust. Or it takes the wrong stand. Or it disagrees with your stand. How do you work within such policies? Is it better to quit or to stay and try to correct the incorrigible? Is your small measure of integrity some contribution to leavening the loaf? Should you strive to rise to a position of authority and responsibility where you can yourself determine policy? You will have these questions.

You will feel uneasy that the whole social function of informing the people is a business, is a function entrusted to business. You are offended that artistry, creativity, and imagination are bought and sold with silver. You feel a kind of desecration in the temple that your ideals and talents are but a means to an 8 per cent return on invested capital. You find that journalism is organized, too. That you belong to a team. That the Macy ad helps to pay your salary. That it takes circulation trucks to speed your prose to the readers breathlessly awaiting. That more attention seems to be paid to hunks of lead than to your immortal soul.

It's all right. Don't change a particle of you. Just be a wee bit philosophic about yourself, about the freedoms that you do have in journalism, and about what organization can do to help you realize your goals.

Journalism and Your Personal Life

Not all the questions you have in journalism will be in-stitutional ones. Some will be entirely personal, and these, too, you need to meet and answer to your satisfaction. There is a turbulence and disorderliness about life in journalism. If you are inclined to be neat, tidy, and orderly about calendars and schedules, you will be unhappy to find that human history has a way of ignoring your lunch hour and nap time. To place the morning's news on the reader's breakfast table means that someone has to work all night. If you are one whose first yawn comes along at about 9:30, you will find it painful to smother it and write another head. If you find pleasure in an easy chair, your slippers, and an evening with the children, not to mention some occasional waking-hour association with your spouse, you are likely to find that putting the paper to bed is no substitute for putting yourself to bed. Too many newspapermen's families have fallen to pieces because of the irregularity of the newspaperman's life.

When you are alone on a story, it is your master. When you are a one-man bureau in a suburban town, you will find irritating the things that those suburbanites can devise to fill twenty-four hours of a day. You can even be bored in this fascinating, exciting life of a journalist. The long hours of waiting, the struggle against sources that insist on bottling up information, sitting through the same kind of weary council meeting for the hundredth time, hearing the same speeches, eating the same chicken-and-peas luncheons—this is excitement?

You will sometimes feel in your associations that you are always the newspaperman and never the person. Occasionally you will feel like a social pariah. Conversations in huddles around the council chamber grow quiet as you approach. Friends and neighbors seem to hear the professional question mark behind even your most innocent inquiries.

Gossips' tongues don't wag quite so fast when you are at the bridge table. It's a lonely vigil, keeping the watch on the foredeck of history.

Confront these problems you have about journalism, within its organizations and within yourself, but don't let them get you down. Confronting them is the first step toward controlling them.

CHAPTER FIVE

In the Process ... Difficulties

In considering a life in journalism you should know the high purposes of your calling, but you should also know the frustrations of those purposes, should come to grips with them and do your best to overcome them. Some of journalism's difficulties come from outside pressures, from the law, from regulation, from the secrecy of sources. But, as we have seen, these are surmountable as long as your case is good and soundly argued before the court of public opinion. Other difficulties come from the process itself . . . the very process for which you bear the ultimate responsibility.

Frustrations of Your High Purposes

You will surely come to entertain doubts about yourself and the profession as well as about the system. You will see half-truths masquerading as the truth. You will wonder how much of the whole story is being discovered, how much told, how much read correctly. You will feel that the institutions you serve are unresponsive to your purpose and that the actors in the drama you report are positively hostile to your efforts. You will watch conspiracies of silence and see the sacred cows of men and institutions; and you will be worried about malproportioning and coloring of the news. The economy of journalism will trouble you, all the way from the size of your pocketbook to the general health of the industry.

You will feel oppressed by the size of the job of communication, maybe even a little downhearted by it. You will seldom be sure that the people are really informed, and this makes the final purpose of your calling a frustration. You will feel ashamed of your superficiality. You will be annoyed at the problem of limited time and limited sources and limited newsprint (or air time). You will know that no one in the business, either yourself or the system, is getting the full story told.

Communication—an Unfinished Business

You will be troubled by the inaudibility of the sound of your own voice. It is difficult to be heard correctly. Communication is an unfinished business. The transfer of ideas, thought, pictures, facts from head to head always involves a percentage loss in exactness. Minds sending and minds receiving are separate and individual minds, and they never quite meet.

Ideally, you hope to convey a composite picture that mirrors your day accurately and in proper proportions. How difficult it is to achieve your ideal. This will be the difficulty that haunts you in journalism. You will find fault and try to place blame, but it is a kind of ultimate frustration. You are in the business of articulating and communicating, and there seems to be a block against complete articulation and communication.

Let's accept this limitation as one of the facts of life and see how close journalism can still come to approaching its ideal. There are controllable factors that affect the accurate and proportioned picture, and so let's see what can be done about them. Some of them are physical. Some are inherent in the customs, forms, and institutions of journalism. Some of the reason that the accurate and proportioned picture does not appear lies at the source; the picture simply does not reveal itself. And some of the reason is in you.

Limitation of Space—a Constant

When William L. Laurence, science reporter for *The New York Times,* wrote for the first time the story of the birth of the atomic age, his editor told him: "Write all you want." It took seven columns of news space, and the editor gave it to him. When John Hersey's manuscript from Japan, called "Hiroshima," arrived in the editorial offices of *The New Yorker* magazine, the entire issue of August 31, 1946, was devoted to printing that manuscript and nothing else. These are unusual occurrences. They were unusual stories, and editorial imagination matched them with unusual treatment.

Physical space in which to present the accurate and proportioned picture is one of the eternal problems of journalism. There is only so much newsprint and only so much time on the air. It can be stated almost categorically that you will *always* feel that you are denied the space that you need to tell the truth, the whole truth, and nothing but the truth about an event you are covering. Limited space is a constant in journalism. When you need four paragraphs to communicate the salient points only, you will be given three. When you have done a decent job and written a column, you will find that the copy editors cut it in two, and it continues to shrink paragraph by paragraph all night long as the editions come and go. On the air, it is even more frustrating to be cramped into a couple of sentences noting the outbreak of war on the Sino-Indian frontier to make way for fifty glittering sentences on Pippitup Liniment.

The limitation of space means that you must learn to walk the tightest rope between too little and too much. You will learn to write economically, simply, tersely, directly. On one side will be the peril of oversimplification; on the other will be the peril of confusing the truth with too many subtleties and qualifications. The limitation of space also means that something has to give, some events have to go uncovered, some stories have to be spiked. Someone has to sit at the gate and exercise selectivity on the elements that are going to compose the picture which mirrors that day in the life of the world. This problem of the gatekeeper will trouble you. Two stories come in. One tells of the technical assistance program of the United Nations in malaria control. The other tells of the dispatch of U.N. troops to the Congo. The Congo story appears, the malaria control story does not appear. What determined the selection? These are decisions of tremendous consequence, and they hold within them the possibilities of distorting the picture of the age. Yet every editor must make them, and make them as responsibly as he can.

The conditions of space are also immutable in respect to relationships in the news. These relationships involve the relative lengths of stories and the positions they occupy in the total presentation. Again, decisions have to be made, decisions that can mean warping and distortion. A blatant public figure makes an injurious charge against a citizen on page one; when the citizen replies, he gets two paragraphs on page 36. When a third of the front page is given over to some special exploit that the newspaper is promoting, with special correspondents and name writers, what happens to the play of the rest of the news of the world? Is "Our Own Girl Reporter" at a luscious murder trial so much more important, relatively, than the news her extravagances push out of the paper? Factors of space and the decisions that are made with the space available are problems always present in journalism, problems that influence the accuracy and proportion of the picture that is being communicated, problems that compromise the ideal.

Limitation of Time

The limitations of time are equally frustrating to perfect communication, and journalism works within a tiny moment on the calendar. "Give me a roundup," the editor says, "on the meaning of 'due process' in law." That's your assignment. And he wants it by noon, two o'clock at the latest. Legal authorities have spent their lives on the meaning of "due process." Books have been written about it. You are expected to ingest all these lifetime works and come up with a readable, accurate, interpretative piece within the duration of a few hours. You will do it. You will learn the knack of quick inquiries, getting to the heart of the matter, paragraphic skimming, riffling an index, getting your mind around a complicated subject in a hurry. But time is a devouring monster, and you will grow to hate him with a passion that is in part a horrible fascination with him.

Newspapermen have been known to wake up sweating from a dream about the DEADLINE. It is a little like being pushed onto the stage to play Macbeth without your clothes on. Newspapers have to be sold, readers have to be told. That means they must receive the paper. That means schedules must be met—trains, buses, airlines. That means the presses must roll, and that means the linotypists and compositors and stereoplaters must produce the material that rolls on the presses. That means the editors must feed the composing room. And that means you must meet a schedule with the raw copy that starts the whole production to move. You will concentrate as you have never concentrated before. Lightning could strike the newsroom and you would never notice. The lead. Snatched away by a copy boy, ripped right out of your typewriter. No turning back. One paragraph after another, each one disappearing into the maw of this waiting monster before it has had a chance to cool. You will probably never become completely inured to the excitement of the deadline.

You will probably sometimes wonder whether all the pressure of time is so necessary, whether time needs to be such an unbending taskmaster in the newsroom. If more time is needed to communicate intelligently, why not take more time? You may occasionally be given all the time you need on a story, but only occasionally. The rule in journalism is to wrap it up in a day, even if the aims and ideals of human communication are frustrated in the process. Perhaps, with competition from radio's and television's speedier journalism, the newspaper will begin to slacken its pace and forsake the deadline psychosis in favor of full and accurate reporting, even if it takes six weeks.

Problems in Journalistic Style

You will also find that some of the forms and traditions of journalism get in the way of the perfect meeting of minds.

Journalistic style itself is so terse and abrupt that one finds little rhetorical beauty, no ornament to the language, and little variety or change of pace as becomes human communication. Listen sometime to the teletypewriter beating out the news of the day; it is symbolic of the monotonous beat which is the percussive instrumentation of all journalism. The form of the news story is so mechanically contrived that it, too, may get in the way of ideal communication. Consider the story that is written backward. Election day. You have come to the close of a brisk campaign. The voters are going to the polls to choose between Candidate A and Candidate B. Obviously, the election is the most important story of the day. But you have nothing to say about it, and so you write that "Detroiters went to the polls today under sunny skies to elect a mayor." The only piece of news in the lead is the sunniness of the skies. Then you review the high points of the campaign, and fill in with biographies of the two candidates rewritten from "Who's Who." About noon you get word that the police have arrested a couple of disturbers of the peace and that a woman in Hamtramck got her finger caught in a voting machine. So you add a paragraph of these momentous facts and insert it below the lead. At eight o'clock you begin to get a smell of the day's story. Candidate A is leading Candidate B by 300 votes in "early and scattered returns." So you write a new lead that conveys that information, move down the sunny skies and the police activities, and finish up with the biographies and the history of the campaign. You see what a patchwork your story is. Can any communicative literature be so contrived? It's astonishing that as much of the news gets across as does soak through. A baseball game at edition time is written the same way—backward.

Consider the tradition of the journalistic lead. A scholar delivers an illuminating and important new analysis of the writings and person of Proust. There are glimpses into his character, there are reflections on the times that produced him, there are brilliant interpretations of his prose. You listen spellbound. Then, in an aside, he comments that Jack Kennedy should have read more of Proust while he was at Harvard. Automatically, you fit yourself to the form. The story is at hand. "A Harvard professor said today that John F. Kennedy should have read more of the writings of Marcel Proust." What happened to the real story? What about the main purpose of the speech? The professor is lucky if he gets a clause somewhere detailing the general theme of his mind. Comments, asides, wisecracks are so much more terse and brittle that they make better lead material than thoughtful discourses.

Professor Theodore Morrison of Harvard once talked over the uncommunicative aspects of journalistic writing with a class of Nieman fellows in Cambridge. He criticized the disjointed, illogical, nonfluid tendencies in journalistic prose. The paragraphs that stand alone, unbridged fore or aft. Sentences so stripped-down that they can't be read for meaning. Prose needs to have the gaps filled in, to flow in measured cadences. There is altogether too much writing of pidgin English in journalism.

"Governor said today Attorney General must go." Not an impossible journalistic sentence, but what does it mean? Does *the* Governor (he is entitled to the definite article) want to fire his chief lawyer? Or send him to Alberta to pick up a prisoner? Or does the sentence mean that the

Attorney General and not the Keeper of the Seal must represent the state at the Liberian Exposition?

Theodore M. Bernstein, assistant managing editor of *The New York Times,* keeps a file of such journalistic ambiguities. If you wish to read a few to your amusement, see his book *Watch Your Language.* A sample: "Waves to Train in Baltimore." Who waves at trains in Baltimore, and why not? Or are the girls of the Navy going to get their training in Baltimore?

Professor Morrison made another point in his critique of journalistic prose: that it broke the rules for a line of expectancy in all writing. Half the job of communication is accomplished if the writer's mind and the reader's mind are working together. There needs to be an expectation in the reader that a certain sentence will follow the sentence that now engages him. He has to have half a notion of where you're going. When you break off, change subjects on him, or leave out too much, or develop your points in an order that defies all logic except the mythical logic of the inverted pyramid, you lose him. He is lost at his point on the page, because he can't remember where he's been and he can't anticipate where he's going.

The logic of journalistic writing is frequently no logic at all. Consider this headline:

COUNCIL BARS
USE OF LAND
FOR HOSPITAL

Turns Down 3 Sisters' Offer,
Also Adds to Police and
Sanitary Forces

Now the article begins:

> The City Council voted last night to turn down the
> offer of the Mandle property on Ridge Road for a new
> city hospital.
>
> In other action in a meeting that lasted until after mid-
> night, the Council also:
>
> —hired three new policemen;

The story continues through a summary of all the actions
taken by the Council. Then, four or five paragraphs later:

> Lawrence D. Brunn, chairman of the Zoning Board,
> was on his feet for nearly an hour before the vote was
> taken that sustained his contention that the new hospital
> should not be placed in a residential area.
>
> "I appreciate the Mandle generosity," he said, "but
> you permit an exception to the zoning ordinances here
> and you can expect to find gas stations in your parlors."

Now we know why the Council acted as it did. The next
paragraph gives the name of the new policemen and other
details of various Council actions. Again:

> The Misses Ethelda, Esmerelda, and Evelinda Man-
> dle, whose home and 20-acre plot were offered to the
> city last May . . .

If you keep after this thing, you may finally begin to piece it
together. This is the logic of journalism. The story is out-
lined according to the best accepted practices in the writing
of multiple incident leads. Write the gist in the headline,
tell it once in the lead, tell it again, then develop the details
as you tell it again.

Examine a simple obituary:

> John Doe, local lawyer, died at his home here yester-
> day after a long illness.
> Born in Illinois, he . . .

The logic of the normal mind would tend to place the birth
of the man before his death. Chronology, the logic of time,
is acceptable in journalism but must never be allowed to
interfere with journalism's own logic.

Recently, a number of journalists have shown concern
over journalistic forms and procedures that by their sheer
weight are tending to obscure communication. Forms and
procedures, which ought to have as their purpose the revealing of the truth, are becoming blocks to the discovery of the
truth. Newsmen and their elaborate attempts to cover a
story are becoming more important than the story itself.
They are intruding upon the formation of the news, instead
of observing it. This problem was noted and discussed by
many of the newsmen who followed the course of Soviet
Premier Nikita Khrushchev on his whirlwind tour of the
United States in 1959. Instead of being a quiet observer,
noting in its pad the progress of the Premier, the press was a
boiling mob that impeded his progress at every turn. He was
burned under the lights of camera crews, entwined in their
cables, surrounded by their ring of insistent questions. He
fought them, used them, and abused them. Was it Khrushchev's tour of America, or Khrushchev *vs.* the press? The
story, the event itself, was conditioned by the presence of
the hundreds of newsmen.

This problem has been enhanced by television news coverage, which comes to its assignment with imposing impedi-
menta, but it is also a logical extension of the forms and

procedures of all journalism. In its zeal to cover a story, the press can smother it, can alter it, can get into the cast of characters of it.

Debates over the presence of cameras and television crews in courtrooms and hearings are related to this problem. Theoretically they would seem to share the same privileges as the print media, but practically they cause such a commotion that they interfere with the course of justice and decorum. Delicate negotiations, if they are invaded by the press, can be destroyed. Newsmen are aware of these dangers and, though they feel compelled to inquire and explore, they are beginning to realize that unless they can be more orderly and restrained about their procedures they run the risk of shaping history rather than reporting it.

"Off-the-Record" Material

Another journalistic form that confuses the public, rather than enlightening it, is the practice in handling off-the-record material and news from the "informed source." A Secretary of State calls three of his favorite reporters and gives them in confidence a detailed summary of the Department's ten-step program for applying sanctions against a troublesome Latin American dictator. This is national policy of a high order and news of first magnitude. The Secretary refuses to let his name be used, although the fact that the information came directly from him is the most important fact about the story. What do the reporters do? In agreeing to listen to the Secretary in confidence they are honor bound to keep the confidence. They feel their public responsibility to make the information known. So they pass along the story and attribute the whole thing to "an unimpeachable source," "a high government official" or some other circumlocutory phrase that covers the identity of the Secretary. The people get the story, but they are robbed of its most important part. Again, the forms and procedures of journalism get in the way of the whole truth rather than facilitating its expression.

Within the institutions of journalism there are also many preconceptions of what is newsy and interesting, assumptions that are never really tested and may conceivably be so out of date that they are no longer true, if they ever were. If a man bites a dog, the formula insists that the action must be recorded in the annals of journalism. On almost all sports pages of the country one can expect to find baseball the leading space consumer. Maybe boating, golf, trampoleaping or tiddledywinks are more interesting to more people than baseball—has anybody checked? Is the formula so sure that the tragic conflicts of an African people to gain statehood are less interesting than the conflicts of a Hollywood playboy against his wives and ex-wives?

In some respects these hallowed formulas of traditional journalism are being mightily shaken in modern practice. People have been discovered in large numbers who will watch a United Nations debate with greater interest than they would have in a football game. Science has come rampaging into journalism over the fallen myth that "such stuff is too highbrow for my simple-minded readers." Exploration, education, religion, housing, recreation, aviation and space, medicine, art—all these and other areas of human experience are making news for modern journalism.

Obstacles on the Road to Truth

Let's construct a hypothetical situation and use it as an illustration of another way in which the truth eludes both the reporter and the reader. You are covering a baseball game, and like most fans you have a favorite team. They are at bat in the last of the ninth, are two runs behind, and are down to their last out. But the bases are loaded and Mr. Bigbat is facing the pitcher. The tension mounts through the proper number of balls and strikes. Suddenly, your hero connects with a cracking sound, and the ball starts on its home-run journey to the centerfield stands. You count the runs as they come thundering across the plate and you begin to write your lead in your mind: "The Blue Sox came from behind in the final minutes today and beat the. . . ." At this point a neighboring reporter says in awestruck tones:

"Never saw such a catch in my life!"

Catch? He fills you in. Gus Glutz, the center fielder, with his back against the wall, leaped and brought down the certain home run, and the game is over. You didn't even see it.

Ponder that story a moment, and see the possibilities in it of a lot of missed truth. How many things don't you see? How many facets of an event escape you? Because you're partisan and biased? Because your mind simply can not conceive of the truth you might uncover if you had the right eyes? Because you can not construct in imagination the questions to ask to expose the truth? It may be that you are not consciously blind or biased. You may not be willfully trying to mislead.

Many newspaper readers have a right to wonder about the full truth of the reports they read. It was difficult for American readers to get into their heads the full import of the advances of Soviet science. Eventually they got the message, but it took a long time. The delay was the fault of no one in particular. The readers had their own prejudices, and reporters and observers reflected the same prejudices. One wonders about the same kind of prejudices and preconceptions that may be coloring our perspective of the news of Red China, Cuba, South Africa, a steel strike, or the integration story. Maybe we are missing the truth because we do not have the eyes to see it or the minds to receive it.

Many of these obstacles on the road to truth are surmountable with a little of your own effort. It is easy for a reporter to become lazy. He begins to know what is expected of him, and he performs up to expectation only. If he has a three-paragraph story to do, and knows that it is all he will get, he asks three questions and lets it go at that. There is really no need to dig into all the facets of a story with four, five, and six questions when you have all you need after a cursory view.

It is easy for a reporter to acquiesce in the closing of sources to him, to file a memo that there is "no story" when a bureaucrat clams up or the mayor refuses to talk. A resourceful rerouting of the questions, a little deeper digging, could have produced the true story.

Suppose that you and a competitor are covering a steel strike. It is in its sixtieth day, negotiations continue, and today is like every other day in the whole two months. So far as you can see, the night's story will be the same old one: "Negotiations continued today without result in the two-month-old steel strike." In fact, your competitor has filed his story, and that is exactly what he wrote.

You are chatting with the room clerk in the hotel where the negotiations continue, and he drops the interesting word that the chief federal mediator has checked out as of 3 P.M. You saunter over to the airlines reservation counter, just to see if the mediator's name might be on a flight to Washington. Sure enough, it is, along with the names of his whole staff and several industry representatives. You check another flight, Pittsburgh bound, and you find that the whole list of union representatives are going out at midnight. Either (1) the negotiations are blowing up completely, or (2) a settlement is scheduled before 11:30. You ask a few discreet questions, and you file your story:

"Peace in the 60-day-old steel strike was near tonight as negotiators continued their talks. 'Could be,' was the response of a union spokesman to a query about the possibility of a pact before midnight."

You are the reporter who looks good a couple of hours later when the negotiators emerge with smiles on their faces and the wire services bulletin the end of the strike. On the routine sixtieth day, you might have relaxed with the routine and the obvious. You made the extra checks, you did the extra work, and the truth came from the extras.

Retroactive Extras

Some of the extras that you can bring to your job are retroactive. You can better reveal the truth about a given Supreme Court decision if you once had a course in constitutional law and have kept up your reading and learning in that field. You can make interesting comparisons on the playing fields if you once memorized what Babe Ruth did or how far Jesse Owens jumped. Simple industry in covering a story is not enough these days. A journalist must have the prepared background that makes the meanings of his story apparent to him. This means that he must be a student, both of humanity in the raw and of humanity's records. He must be a man of learning, rich and deep. He must have acquired learning, and he must have the instincts to keep on learning.

The communications barriers might come crashing down with more extras on the part of you. Extra effort, extra attention, extra imagination, extra exertion of your conscience. When time and space run you ragged, and you know in your heart that the communicative job has not been done, you can write an interpretative piece for the week end that draws together the strands which looked like confusion in the heat of the day. Spend an hour a week sitting alone with your prejudices; see how they look under X ray. Try this test: read a story you have written and measure each fact and assumption in it alongside its opposite. Does this reveal any false assumptions, any possibility of other facts? Would your story seem fair to one whose assumptions were diametrically opposed to yours?

Study this illustration. Here is a snatch from something you have written:

> Snarling like a cornered dog, he hugged a corner of his cell. Police said he was trapped on the roof of the building where the body was found when they took him. He resisted at first, but was quietly surly this morning after a night of police questioning.

There are assumptions in that paragraph, perhaps dangerous ones. You are assuming much in favor of the police. You suggest guilt. You subtly color the character of the man. Now, reverse gears and take a new set of assumptions. See what turns out:

> Police reached into a grab-basket yesterday to produce someone who could be involved in the Johnson

slaying. After a night of being bludgeoned by questions, Legrow seemed to be the likeliest candidate to date. . . .

End of the illustration. The point is clear. It is up to you to find the way to truth through these facts and, without assumptions and preconceptions, lead the reader to it.

If journalistic style and story forms don't communicate, invent some new ones. If you think the man-bites-dog formula is confining, and if you can write to interest readers about bowling, or about the Dead Sea scrolls, or about what's being done for retarded children, or about what goes on in the minds of a Schweitzer, a Conant, an Oppenheimer, a Barzun, you will have no difficulty with your editor. Strangely enough, he, too, is interested in writing to interest readers. If you find that you are invading the news under the pretense of reporting it, lengthen your perspective, organize your coverage, keep it under observation, but get out of the act.

Yes, the picture is frequently half-true and distorted. But there are many things that you can do to set it right, and when you can't, you will keep trying anyway, impelled by a thrust from outside for which the theologians have many terms and the journalists, vivid experience.

CHAPTER SIX

From the Endeavor . . . Authenticity

Journalism is traditionally an exciting pursuit. Each assignment means a new experience, new people to meet. There is a certain freedom from the rigidity and discipline of corporate life. There is the satisfaction of being privy to the news before it is news, of watching history being made. You are a generalist rather than a specialist and have freedom to rove that another does not have who is tied by his talent to a single body of knowledge or experience. The scientist rejoices in his achievement, and you share in his satisfaction by communicating the word of it. The lawyer, the statesman, the center fielder, all have their jobs to do and successes to score, and you become part of them as you record their deeds. In journalism the pace is fast, the variety is as wide as all experience, and accomplishment is swift and neatly packaged at each day's end. These and other attractions have certainly influenced you as you have considered your response to the call of journalism.

Always the Viewer of History

But the very freedom of your position, the liberty to roam and observe and share in the experiences of others will sometimes make you feel cut off, adrift, unmoored, suspended in human history without any roots in it. Always the bridesmaid, never the bride. Always the viewer of history, while others make and move it. In his book *The Washington Correspondents*,[1] Leo Rosten gives terse expression to this feeling. "Reporters derive a vicarious pleasure in experiencing the excitement of events as observers, not participants, without personal risk in the outcome of those events." This suggests faintly a rather parasitic role for the journalist, detached and remote, uninvolved in the processes of history and the decisions that make it up. You will feel at times that Mr. Rosten is right. You will watch stouthearted decisions being made—for instance, a vote to send troops to Korea—and you will feel relieved that you did not have to cast your ballot. Relieved, but a little guilty at the same time. You are not in the ring, taking the blows and dishing them out. You are watching from afar. You are not producing an original economic good, like a Ford car or a head of lettuce. You are merely an observer of the rest of society's economic production.

Sometimes you will feel a bit irresponsible in the way you heckle. Working out your hostilities under the aegis of journalistic duty is the way that Mr. Rosten psychoanalyzes your behavior. Without putting pencil to drafting board, you criticize the lines of the new Ford car. Without planting a seed or turning a spade, you write in your food column that Carolina lettuce is wormy this year. You paint a picture of the party whip in the legislature, storming, threatening, coaxing, trading votes, a picture that purposely makes the man look bad to your readers, and he's only doing his assigned job without which the legislative wheels would not roll. You criticize the traffic department for its lack of control of the number of cars on the street, and your convertible is outside, up against a fireplug with a press privilege card stuck in the windshield. You can analyze everything wrong that the sit-in demonstrator did, but he made his choice, took his stand, and did something. Is Mr. Rosten right that you tend to build up hostilities when you are continually frustrated as a participant in history, and therefore you project your hostilities by heckling what everybody else does? If you can't eat hay, then you'll sleep in the manger to make sure the horse doesn't.

"The Fourth Estate"

Alongside Mr. Rosten's book, read *The Fourth Branch of Government* [2] by Douglass Cater, another book that comments on the role of the press in Washington. You will get a different view. Mr. Cater believes that journalism is a positive force and plays a decision-making role in government. Instead of being aloof and uninvolved, the press is an active participant in history. It influences decisions all the time, brings the power of the people to bear upon government, and interprets government to the people. Even in its role of responsible critic, it initiates and creates and influences the events of history.

One recognizes in this description of the role of the press the familiar phrase out of the century just past, "the fourth estate." Lord Macaulay wrote in 1828: "The gallery in which the reporters sit has become a fourth estate of the realm." He meant almost precisely what Mr. Cater means: that the

press functions with political power at the seat of government and suffers the consequences of its exercise of power.
The picture of the observer that Mr. Rosten paints may look
frighteningly familiar at times, and as such is good for the
soul, but the truth is that the journalist has his feet wet in
the stream of history and asks for no one to throw him his
galoshes.

Reporters Objective, Politicians Subjective

The ways of exercising power are different. The reporter
did not get elected from the third Congressional district to
cast votes in the House of Representatives. The voters can
not throw him out. But this does not mean that the reporter
should curl up and die because he's not a Congressman.
Gifts are different, ways to contribute to political action are
different; but the contribution is made effectively all the
same. When the press exposed the Tweed ring in New York
City, did it not make decisions in the political arena for that
city? When a simple, clean, and communicative report is
written of an important municipal action, does not the reporter march with history by his act of informing the people? So he doesn't grow cabbages; the reporter still contrib-
utes valuably to the economy of men's lives.

The feeling of detachment, which Mr. Rosten wrote about
and which many reporters are troubled about, probably
stems from the way a journalist participates in history. His
whole effort is to objectify it; the active politician, the so-
called history maker, always subjectifies it. The politician,
therefore, gets a feeling of commitment, of immediacy, of
attachment that a reporter can never have. This is not to
say, however, that the reporter has any less of a role in poli-

tics and history. Indeed, he may have more, because he has freedoms and disinterest that a politician does not have.

The press is enormously relevant to all our history, our politics, our government. Our form of society could not operate without the press—is that too much to say? If there were no press to mediate between people and state, something else in a democracy would have to be invented to inform, to watch and criticize, to arm and stimulate the public debate. "Were it left to me to decide," Thomas Jefferson once said, "whether we should have a government without newspapers or newspapers without a government, I should not hesitate a moment to prefer the latter." He knew that responsible and responsive popular government had to have the press as the people's mouthpiece, eyepiece, and earpiece.

There have been political correspondents who have maintained that they never voted. Hearing them, you may inquire: "Do I have to quit being a citizen in order to be a journalist?" The answer is no. But there are reservations upon your political activity that may at times look like a curtailment of active citizenship. The point is partisanship. To keep your effectiveness as a journalist, and as a citizen who is at the same time a journalist, you can not be too active a joiner, you can not be publicly partisan, you can not obligate yourself to one or the other of the parties to the dialogue of whatever spot in history you are covering. The ballot box is secret, and for your purposes it would better stay that way. Your political service is to keep your objectivity and your disinterest, and it is no less a political service. If this objectivity is too much for you, and your civic duty calls you to get onto the hustings and into print in behalf of one party, then you would better take a leave of absence as a journalist and go to work as an effective publicist for the party of your choice.

Conflict of Interest—a Danger

On the subject of joining, some other things must be said. In any kind of conflict story, you must make sure that you don't have a conflict of interest. It's bad enough in Assistants to the President, but it's worse in you. Politics, strikes and labor negotiations, court cases, sports, economic competition, debates and conflicts of all kinds—in covering areas like these you must not be so precommitted to one side in the conflict that you lose your objectivity and your usefulness and obscure the pursuit of truth.

If your Republican sympathies are well known, if you are a close friend and lunching companion (on him) of the majority leader in the state senate, if you are a paid consultant to the county committee or an unpaid talebearer who favors the Republican team, no Democrat will talk to you. You have lost your usefulness to your newspaper and to the people who are counting on you for a balanced, objective, fair account. It may be that you have pronounced Republican sympathies, but you must keep the respect and confidence of both parties. It is good practice to accept favors from neither principal in a conflict situation. Pick up your own check at lunch. Send back the gifts. Suppose you are covering a campaign in which the Republicans have a skeleton in the closet that no one has yet mentioned. You know about it, but there is a chance that the Democrats are not aware of it, or else they do not know its significance. It is important enough to warrant public debate, and to expose it would be the sensation of the campaign. Now what do you do? The majority leader has you in his pocket, and he would get hurt. The Democrats haven't found the issue; should you hand it to them on a platter? Should you hide the skeleton and thus be party to suppressing the news, journalism's capital offense? Which comes first, the public interest or the party interest?

The same kinds of questions can be raised through all the reportorial ranks. Should the labor reporter belong to the Guild? Should he belong to the National Association of Manufacturers? Should the religion reporter belong to any one church or denomination? Should the sports reporter do publicity for a local bowling alley as a sideline? What should be all reporters' attitudes toward and relationships with all publicity agents? Should the reporter who covers housing take a paid publicity job with the nonprofit Committee for Better Housing? Should the education reporter do publicity consulting for the National Education Association? Or the science reporter for the American Medical Association? You're the man who covers football. The local college calls you in and asks if you would take four hours of work each week to run the college sports publicity office. How about it? Do the interests conflict?

The answers to these questions vary. Some reporters make a hard and fast rule and refuse to identify themselves with any organization that has a stake in the fruits of publicity and promotion. Some reporters would distinguish and find clear conflicts of interest in some cases and none in others. Sometimes institutional policy will answer the questions for you. At issue is your own independence and objectivity. When you trade the people's eyes and ears for a special-interest pair, you are being unfaithful to a trust. You have a professional discipline as a journalist, and it will make you extraordinarily alert to pressures and conflicts. You will know immediately when someone is trying to buy you or influence your function as a journalist. Join whatever you want to join. The important thing is to recognize for what they are the pressures, the assumptions and preconceptions within you, the special interests, and never to let them interfere with the search for truth as zealously as you are able to pursue it.

To Accept or Not to Accept Gifts?

Related to this problem is the bothersome one of how far you should go in accepting gifts. This is a tough one. It is customary practice for many organizations to send gifts to their friends of the press at holiday times. An appliance manufacturer sends along one of his samples. A food distributor thinks well enough of you to invite you to accept an offering of gastronomical delights. Bottled goods move with especial celerity. Business picks up noticeably in the pen-and-pencil set department. All this Christmas "loot" is matched with free passes, discounted tickets, travel, lodging, free meals, and drinks all the year round.

To quote again from Bob Estabrook: "The airlines which offer free inaugural trips, the automobile manufacturers who offer cars at cut rates to newspapermen, the industries which establish 'honors' and 'awards' for the press may be doing it all for the love of humanity, but somehow I doubt it. Suspicious fellow that I am, I think that they are doing it because they want to create a favorable public relations climate. They would be insulted at the suggestion that they were attempting to buy the press, but the newspapermen who accept such private perquisites at least create a presumption that they are open to purchase." [3]

The public was scandalized recently (and the newspapers

were singularly wroth) to learn of the payola practices in television. Manufacturers were paying to have their records "plugged" on musical shows, a practice that has more recently been prohibited by law. How far apart are payola in television and the acceptance of "loot" on the newspapers?

There are many ways to meet this problem. Some newspapermen refuse to accept any gifts or favors. Some institutions prohibit the practice among their employees. Some persons will accept a gift under certain conditions, depending upon its size, the relationship to the giver, the sincerity of the intent in giving. Some corporations and agencies have ceased to send gifts to newspapermen and send instead a note that reads: "At this holiday season we thought you would like to know that we have made a contribution in your name to the local orphanage," or some other charitable enterprise. To be honest, some newspapermen take everything that's sent.

The critical point is what happens to you in the process. Journalists have enough of a reputation as free loaders, as it is. They don't need any more addition to the reputation from you. Earlier in this book some points were made about the relationship between advertisers and the press, about pressures that advertisers might or might not bring upon the editorial content and opinion of newspapers, about the necessity for integrity, independence, and objectivity among the institutions of journalism. The points are exactly the same when you put yourself individually in the way of pressures from the special interests who come bearing gifts. Take an occasional free ticket or gift, if you want to, but don't become a free loader, a known collector of perquisites, ready to jump at every junket, blatantly announcing yourself as "for sale." Your integrity, independence, and objectivity are as important as your institution's. In fact, they're of a piece.

Exploiting the Emotions

You will be sitting at your desk someday, bemoaning your place on the sidelines of history, when an assignment will land there that will suddenly sweep you up into history in a most unnerving way. This is the assignment that takes you into the presence of pathos, tragedy, grief, anger. Now you are no longer the disinterested observer. You are embarrassingly involved in humankind. You will even cry a little, feel the tug in your throat, grope for words, feel your own jaw set in anger. Your involvement may be only embarrassment, but most reporters, even experienced ones, dread the day that they have to intrude upon grief. Some have actual conscientious objection, at points in covering a story, to exploiting the emotions in it any further. Something within them rebels at asking one more question or staying one more minute. This is an experience that every reporter has had, and he doesn't like it.

It is not easy, but it's not impossible. You have before you the police report that three teen-agers have been killed in an automobile smash-up a dozen miles away. The widowed mother of one lives in your town. Her name is there in the telephone directory, right in front of you. You dial clumsily, knowing what is ahead of you. She is on the telephone, and you have the awful duty of telling her of the accident and in the presence of her grief asking the questions you need to ask. How do you do it? Sometimes reporters, probably to compensate for their embarrassment, become cold and abrupt and forget they are human beings. This is no time for the bad manners of a Scoopy Jones or Flashy Smith.

You are with this mother in one of the memorable moments of her life. You hold in your custody her deepest and innermost feelings. You behave yourself quietly, sympathetically, reassuringly. You can actually help this woman, as a friendly neighbor who drops in, or as pastor or priest.

Waiting at the top of mine shafts, identifying the dead in a makeshift morgue, moving among the griefstricken at a mass disaster, counting down the minutes at an execution, checking out the casualty lists from the battlefronts, writing sketches of the dead in an airplane crash, keeping the watch outside surgery or with two anguished parents in a kidnaping—these are the tough assignments. You will meet hysterics, incoherence, the dumbness of the numbed. You will wonder whether it is really so important that the public be informed when every question rips a wound. You will feel that some emotions are too private to be shared. But grief is human and universal, and in the context of the Christian faith it is even a channel of healing. Man's interest in it is not necessarily invasive and impersonal; it can be warm and sympathetic. Most of man's most noble efforts—metaphysical, physical, medical, social—have been born in sympathetic response, in a desire to do something to assuage grief and pain.

If you are offended at yourself, your incivility, your bad manners, your insensitive intrusions into the privacies of others there is less cause for alarm than if you have grown so cold and insensitive that you stalk through a morgue with no more twinge than you would feel inside a museum. If you are bothered by questions that sound inhuman in even your own ears, be glad that your ears are still able to sense their inhumanity. When you wade through other persons' grief and misery to get your story, be alarmed only if

you sense no grief and share no concern. If all considerations on earth seem secondary to getting your story and
printing it, be concerned only if the story feeds the curiosity
of men without also eliciting their sympathy and response.
At the center of human experience the element of tragedy
stands like a stark symbol of men's common lot, and elicits
a common response of concern and support. To outline the
symbol in a way that elicits the response is to deepen the
dimensions of human life until, because they hurt, they also
heal.

Motivations in Journalists

In assessing career motivation in journalists, two responses seem fairly consistent as persons in the profession
state their reasons for entering it. "I wanted to write." That's
one. "I wanted to observe and work with people and understand them, and journalism seemed, for me, the best place
to do those things satisfactorily." That's the other. Bring up
the subject sometime in a bull session around a newsroom,
and you will hear these responses stated in varying ways.
You will also hear some others, but wanting to write and
wanting to work with people are always constant.

"I suppose I wanted to be some kind of leader in my community, and journalism was the best and quickest way for
me to get to that position."

"I get some ego satisfaction, some sense of power, out of
being 'ahead of the event,' being first with the information that everyone else must have to be enlightened and
intelligent."

"Law and medicine were not for me. Either my talents
did not run in those directions, or I chose not to go through

the necessary disciplines to be licensed in them. Hence, here I am in journalism."

"An accident only. My uncle wanted me to be a lawyer. My mother wanted me to go into Wall Street. But my father owned the newspaper. So here I am in journalism."

"I like to chase fire engines and romp around with exciting events and exciting people. I suppose I don't want to grow up. I want to play with life without getting too involved in it."

As everyone undresses his psyche, you will hear comments like these. Almost always, however, the motivations will return to the desire to write and the need for some kind of relationship of power to other people. There is certainly something in a journalist that compels him to express himself with the written word. Whereas other people may express themselves manually, or artistically, or athletically, or orally, your inclination is to sit at your typewriter, summon up your thoughts and your argument, and go to work with written forms to express yourself.

Though this is a somewhat lone-wolf posture, your fascination with the ways mankind behaves places you back in the mainstream of social and political life. You want to understand people, how they function, what compels them, what they are individually, and what are the forces that drive them in their groups and institutions.

Now examine those motivations. Aren't we really saying that every journalist in his heart wants to be (1) a novelist or (2) a politician? Or both? If you scratch a journalist, you are likely to find that he will confess both these secret desires. He probably has a novel in the typewriter at home. He probably is fooling around on the edges of politics. Everyone knows that Henry Beetle Hough, a newspaperman, produces a steady stream of novels. It is not hard to recall *Advise and Consent*,[4] the product of a Washington newsman. You know that Henry Cabot Lodge began his career as a newspaper reporter, and that President Harding was a publisher from Marion, Ohio. The names of William Allen White, Blair Moody, Senator Knowland, Ernest Hemingway, and A. B. Guthrie, Jr., will also come to mind. You can not fail to note the coinciding of interests among journalists, novelists, and politicians.

The implications in this unraveling of motivations will disturb you occasionally. You will wonder about how serious and dedicated you are toward your calling. Is journalism a value in itself, or is it merely a temporary situation on the road to something else? If your innermost desire is to be a novelist, why are you fooling around in journalism? Get an attic and go to work on your novel. If you really want to wield the power of politics, why hang around in the press gallery? Find a precinct and get to work.

But, you will say, the motivations are more complicated than that. "I don't really want to be a novelist. I don't think I can be a novelist. I don't think I know enough about life. I need to see more of it. Furthermore, I've got to earn a living, and journalism is a way to keep eating while I observe life and people and prepare for the Great American Novel I may someday write."

All this confession makes journalism sound like a second-class occupation. Others may aspire to and achieve the virtuoso ranks, but you have contented yourself with playing second fiddle. It is your lot to be the hack. You dwell with the commonplace. Posterity (a generally disagreeable group) will not remember you. All this is somewhat sad and wasteful, but there you are, stuck with your second choice, a member of the supporting cast.

The same complications exist with those of you who have a lust for politics. "Not really," you will say. "I like it here on Mount Olympus where I can fire my thunderbolts in all directions and be safe about it. Too many compromises if you get into the heat of political maneuvering. I can be tidier and more idealistic from my distance. I love politics, but the road is too long and too rough to get into it. My way is a short cut to get close to the seats of the mighty, if never to sit there myself."

Again, one feels the hints of second-class status. Others may rise to power, make the decisions, and take the credit or blame for them, touch history and leave their mark upon it. You are writing a descant to the main melodic line, fiddling away in the alto section. You echo their pronouncements and record their decisions. They are the stars. You're a member of the junior varsity.

Leo Rosten, whose book was introduced with a quotation a number of pages ago, sums up these motives that place the journalist close to but apart from the politician. He mentions "the desire to startle and expose" and "the opportunity to project personal hostilities and feelings of injustice on public persons under the aegis of 'journalistic duty,'" and he speaks of "the inner drives for 'action,' plus inner anxieties about accepting the consequences of action."

"There is a sense of invulnerability attached to newspaper work," Mr. Rosten writes. "Journalism represents a world within a world. Reporters derive a vicarious pleasure in experiencing the excitement of events as observers, not participants, without personal risk in the outcome of those events." [5]

The long road through law school, or seminary, and the longer one through medical school, the intensity of specialization, the cramming and the books, the expense—you may look at these requirements and conclude that journalism is the "easiest" profession to get into. (Again, the alto violin.) The license to practice journalism is free, both in fact and in law, and journalism is a comfortable route to professional status. This could conceivably be another thought to give you an anxious moment about the kind of detour you are taking into life.

Journalism—No Second-Choice Calling

The fact that these questions and doubts exist is important, and no one dismisses them lightly. But they are a kind of introspective brooding that avails little and does not need to be. Journalism is not a second-choice calling. It plays accompaniment to no one's starring role. It stands on its own solid trunk, rooted in noble traditions and bringing forth its own good fruit in season.

Consider this hack literature that you produce. "Journalism," says Louis Lyons, "requires a lean, muscular prose that marches on strong verbs to clear, precise statement of facts." That's a nice sentence. Novelists should deserve as much. Indeed, the crisp, virile, natural prose of journalism has become normative for the age of letters that we live in. Read Hemingway, Dos Passos, the war novelists, most of the belle of belles-lettres. Their stylistic mark is journalistic. Who's copying whom? Who's playing first violin, anyhow? As you would summarize the cycles of English style from Chaucer to the present, from plain to ornate, you would have to classify modern literature as plain, blunt, Anglo-Saxon, journalistic. The penny-a-liner in the newsroom has had some influence upon the literature of his day. Many journalists, sticking close to their own craft in method and approach, have been turning out some of the century's best work in history. Allan Nevins, Douglas Southall Freeman, Roy F. Nichols, Hodding Carter, Bruce Catton, and Herbert Agar are the names of only a few from a multitude.

John Ciardi, in an essay to writers, discusses what they must learn and some of the elementary functions they must perform. Devotion to the fact is one of the demands he makes upon a writer. Mentioning Robert Frost, he writes:

"His own poems are full of stunning examples of the central truth that good writers deal in information, and that even the lofty acreages of poetry are sown to fact." He then quotes the opening lines of Frost's "Mending Wall," and adds these words:

"I intend no elaborate critique of this passage. I want simply to make the point that it contains as much specific information about stone walls as one could hope to find in a Department of Agriculture pamphlet. . . .

"Consider Melville's passion for the details of whaling," he goes on, "or Defoe's for the details of criminality, of ransoming an English merchant captured by a French ship, or of Robinson Crusoe's carpentry." [6]

Good writers have always dealt with fact and information, and a journalist needs feel no shame that he deals with the same things. A scrivener, detailing in the heat of the day the facts of a town budget, is engaged in no different work from that of a Hemingway, putting down in intricate detail the facts about a mountain pass in the Guadarrama range.

The last word, and a delightful word, in defense of the "journalistic craft" has been said by Alistair Cooke in his foreword to the *Bedside Guardian,* an anthology of daily journalistic pieces put together from the pages of the *Manchester Guardian.* If you feel troubled about your second-class status as a writer of the news, you should read the whole foreword. He writes:

> There is a very odd and enduring contradiction between the prejudice of the intelligentsia that today's journalism is a debased form of literature and history and the steady belief of historians that yesterday's journalism is one of the most authentic of documentary sources. . . .
>
> Yet the sensitive hacks scraping a living between the definitive biography or the Big Novel keep on telling us that journalism is one of the enemies of promise and that nothing dissipates the mobilizing of one's best energies so much as the thousand-word dispatch, the five-hundred-word review, the fifteen-minute broadcast. Meanwhile, the historians (who privately share this contempt for journalists alive and kicking) go on salvaging, as precious artifacts of dead cultures, Defoe's account of fish-curing at Bideford, W. H. Russell's dispatches from the American Civil War, Pepys on almost everything from the taste of an indifferent dinner to the glance of a pretty girl in church.
>
> There is a strong strain of snobbery in this. . . . Pepys and Defoe, after all, were hardly literature in their day. One was a fussy gossip, the other a time-serving pamphleteer, a hind let loose. Yet, like all good journalists, they kept their eyes on the object, and today no synthetic historical account of the Great Plague, put together from no matter how many contemporary documents, can compete in dreadful accuracy with Defoe's jottings in his

journal about a teen-age girl moaning in an alley-way or a desperate father scrawling the fateful cross on his front door. . . .

My argument against the Enemies of Promise mourners must be, then, that either they cannot recognize one species of literature on the wing but must wait for it to be pinned and classified and preserved in amber; or that they are ignorant of the peculiar and demanding craft of journalism, in an age which is, above all preceding others, the age of the journalist.[7]

Mr. Cooke then invites the reader's attention to the pieces that will follow in the anthology:

Let us use them to honor the writer who must say what is on his mind against the twilight's deadline, the professional scribbler who stands or falls by his ability to see clearly and to write fast, and who must learn to overcome the nagging self-conceit of the "serious" full-time writer, whose "craven scruple of thinking too precisely on the event" is too often rationalized as an itch for perfection.[8]

Comparing "the 'serious' novelist or biographer in his cloister and the reporter filing his daily dispatch, sometimes with the wind of the world in his face," Mr. Cooke goes on:

The disparity between the quality of their stuff is still no more or less than that between two men of different talent; it has very little to do with the accidental binding of one man's pieces into a book and the scattering of the other man's pieces into a hundred issues of his paper. . . .

My main point is that journalism is good and bad; it is not bad because it is journalism but because it is

abominably written; that is to say, its material is tritely
observed, crudely felt, and foggily communicated. The
same may be said of a great many medical papers, historical monographs, and nearly all sociological treatises.
In truth, the journalist is merely the scapegoat of all
professionals who put pen to paper.[9]

You should feel some reassurance in Mr. Cooke's picture of the newsman, "against the twilight's deadline," and
"with the wind of the world in his face," batting out his
snatch of literature, his moment of history.

The late Meyer Berger, reporter extraordinary for *The
New York Times*, when sent to cover a funeral, came back
with a snatch of literature and a moment of history. He
wrote:

> The first war dead from Europe came home yesterday.
> The harbor was steeped in Sabbath stillness as they
> came in on the morning tide in 6,248 coffins in the hold
> of the transport Joseph V. Connolly.
>
> One coffin, borne from the ship in a caisson, moved
> through the city's streets to muffled drumbeats and slow-
> cadenced marches, and 400,000 New Yorkers along the
> route and at a memorial service in Central Park paid it
> the tribute of reverent silence and unhidden tears.
>
> The transport Joseph V. Connolly broke through the
> haze outside the Narrows at 9 A. M., a shadowy hulk all
> gray and tan, with a funeral wreath at her forepeak.
> Nothing moved on her decks. The coffin picked out for
> the service, guarded by men at attention, was out on the
> boat deck. . . .[10]

And so the reporter went on through the facts and details,
the feelings and moods, to tell his story of the return of the

war dead from Europe. Flecked with poetry, hints of alliteration and the long dactylic measures of the slow, dirgelike march, the story marshaled its facts and performed its communicative job in a cloak of beauty. No writer on earth could wish for more than that.

Most of these self-doubts and questions about career and motivations, about involvement and detachment, are part of a basic dilemma to which the Christian journalist may be peculiarly well equipped to bring some light and understanding. The journalist is, almost always, afflicted with a marked swelling of the ego. The disease is related to his career choice of journalism in the first place. Mention has been made of numbers of ways this overactive ego intrudes on the routines of the journalistic life. The Christian journalist has to live with his disease. And it's difficult, because he keeps remembering a lot of basic things about the self— about humility, about acts of reverence, about the meek. He can't realize without a great deal of personal torment that he stands under an order to find his life by losing it. The journalist is always tempted to feed his ego. There is a temptation to stop at nothing to get the story, even though other human beings are injured or destroyed in the process. Journalism can sometimes be seen as a craft that lacks even simple codes of decency. Its arrogance, incivility, insensitivity, and occasional brutality do not go unnoticed. Writers have been known to twist the facts and embroider them when such behavior makes for purpler prose, a better story. They have worn blinders in the presence of the facts. They have been known to hear only what they want to hear and to refuse to see what they subjectively do not want to see. Their own self-force in the chronicles of man has sometimes been more powerful than the force of fact, logic, and truth. The journalist frequently deals with elements in history that tend to hurt and destroy others who are caught in the web of life beside him. He is often tempted to take upon himself the role of avenging angel and say, "I hurt, I accuse, and I destroy."

Journalism has a few of its own correctives against such unbridled ego-thrusts. It is a communicative business, and communication involves community. The writer who prefers only to express himself has little usefulness in communicative journalism. He stops to dance a jig on the communications bridge—and only interrupts the flow of traffic across it.

The image of the Lord, who though in the form of God did not grasp after divinity, but "emptied himself" and took on the form of a servant, is an image that profoundly unsettles one who likes his power, his vanity, and the sound of his own voice.

CHAPTER SEVEN

At the End . . . a Word

When you immerse yourself in the forms and disciplines of journalism, and strive to work out a vocation from God inside that profession, watch yourself. There are some risks involved. Anyone who takes on a lay ministry in the secular world may find himself becoming less a minister and more a creature of the secular world that possesses him. It is easy to be taken in by the norms and standards that govern that world.

Standards of Excellence—Not Enough

Journalism, like all other professions, has standards of excellence. Good as they are, they are not enough. That is the perspective you should bring to your field. You must always have a measure of judgment upon your profession that comes from beyond the profession itself. It is your avenue for serving God and your fellow men, and never an end in itself.

Accuracy, clarity, force, and the beauty of your prose are estimable goals. But they are not enough. You are more than a merchant of words. You are a compassionate, searching person, trying with the powers that are in you to lead your fellow men to understanding and truth.

Even the Truth—Not Enough

Even the truth is not enough. You should become known in your shop as the gadfly with the endless questions: How do you know this is true? How can you be sure? Is this the real truth or only the truth that we have conditioned ourselves to see and hear? Truth is an elusive thing, and that is what keeps the search going. The error of all ideology is that it comes too swiftly and too simply to the truth. You should know this, and always strive to keep your journal with its eyes narrowed for the more distant truth.

In early 1961, after the tragic death of the Congolese leader, Patrice Lumumba, numbers of American Negroes expressed their frustrations, hostility, and grief in demonstrations inside and outside the United Nations chambers in New York. The wildness of the demonstrations stunned America. Suddenly the American people were confronted with a new fact, a poison in their system, a defection, a criticism of the accepted American position that cried out for understanding. The journalists had their jobs to do in covering this explosion at the United Nations. They described the event itself, the surface of the happening. Journalistic cameras took a photographic image to the television audience. Many of the demonstrators were given their chance to speak up before the press and camera. At the end of that troubled day, the world knew with considerable factual accuracy what had happened. And when the editorial writers and the commentators moved to bring their voices to bear upon the demonstration, the editorial voice was almost uniform. People should behave themselves. Irrational, emotional, savage—these were the words of condemnation that rang from the editorial chambers. Rioting was deplored. The police force should be strengthened. The whole event was being passed off that second day as a massive mistake, a deplorable disturbance of the peace.

Why did it happen? What was the meaning of the event? What were the hidden truths that rose to the surface of expression that tragic day? These were the questions that lingered as the elusive truth remained uncovered. Two days later, the columnists, commentators, interpreters, and editorialists had caught their breath and were pressing the search for understanding. A whole new complex of truth emerged. Thousands of words were written and spoken as journalism began to dig into the recesses behind this story —the surge of black nationalism, the thrust of colored persons into the power struggles of the world, the sympathies and identifications of frustrated American Negroes, the neuroses that fester in a democracy that is reluctant to practice democracy. These were some of the problems toward which journalism turned its probing mind in those early days after a seething volcano erupted in American society and made visible a host of questions that demanded true answers. The search for those true answers will go on, and you should be glad to have a part in pressing it forward.

An Instrument for a More Just Society

Taking seriously your vocation, you should have extraordinary contributions to bring to your profession as an instrument for a more just society. You should know with precision when and how and where to throw the weight of your journal into the tactical struggles for fairness in human relations. You should not be cynical and defeated by the tragedies of injustice. Some things, after all, are more just than others—the tragedy helps to illuminate your understanding of this fact—and they are the things to which you set yourself. The deeper is your understanding of the reality of injustice in human history, the higher and wiser and more vital is your hope.

"What Do Ye More Than Others?"

The question remains at the end of a book like this: "What do ye more than others?" It is hard to answer. You are a person, of course, and it is assumed that you will have disciplines of personality that mark you as Christian in your relationships to God, your home, your community. These relationships are constant, whatever your daily work. But it has been one's daily work that has been under the spotlight in these pages. In it, "what do ye more than others"? You certainly do not do less than any other in responding to the demands of the profession itself. Nothing in your accepting a vocation from God excuses you from the fullest realization of your potential in talents and skills. You give them, unreservedly, for the most excellent journalistic practice of which you are capable. Incentives toward professional excellence, and unwillingness to relax in standards that are less than excellent, are ways in which you will show your sense of vocation.

Perhaps you will understand more deeply than some of your colleagues the realities of your profession—its demands, its satisfactions, its internal problems, its pressures, its stern necessities, its ideals, and its failures. It can be

hoped that as you encounter these realities, you will find re-
sources in your faith to help you deal with them imaginatively and effectively. It may be that precisely at the point
where these encounters are most difficult, you will find your
daily work most meaningful, you will sense most keenly its
importance in human history, and you will feel most deeply
God's presence in it.

Notes by Chapter

Chapter One: In the Beginning . . . the Word

1. E. B. White, *The Elements of Style* (New York: The Macmillan Company, 1959).

2. Jessamyn West, *To See the Dream* (New York: Harcourt, Brace and Company, 1956).

Chapter Three: The Ambiguous Base . . . Freedom

1. From *Areopagitica, a Speech of Mr. John Milton for the Liberty of Unlicensed Printing, to the Parliament of England; a pamphlet,* Nov. 25, 1644.

Chapter Six: From the Endeavor . . . Authenticity

1. Leo Rosten, *The Washington Correspondents* (New York: Harcourt, Brace and Co., 1937). By permission.

2. Douglass Cater, *The Fourth Branch of Government* (Boston: Houghton Mifflin Co., 1959).

3. In Mr. Estabrook's recent address at the University of Michigan.

4. Allen Drury, *Advise and Consent* (New York; Doubleday & Co., Inc., 1959).

5. See Note 1 of this chapter.

6. John Ciardi, in *Saturday Review,* Dec. 15, 1956. By permission.

7. *Bedside Guardian* (New York: Ives Washburn, Inc., © 1959). By permission.

8. *Ibid.*

9. *Ibid.*

10. *New York Times,* Oct. 27, 1947. By permission.

Haddam House Books

Primer for Protestants   James Hastings Nichols
Youth Asks About Religion   Jack Finegan
Young Laymen—Young Church   John Oliver Nelson
The Human Venture in Sex, Love, and Marriage

Peter A. Bertocci
Science and Christian Faith   Edward LeRoy Long, Jr.
Rediscovering the Bible   Bernhard W. Anderson
The Unfolding Drama of the Bible   Bernhard W. Anderson
The Student Prayerbook

John Oliver Nelson and Others, Editors
Community of Faith   T. Ralph Morton
Politics for Christians   William Muehl
The Paradoxes of Democracy

Kermit Eby and June Greenlief
The Tragic Vision and the Christian Faith

Nathan A. Scott, Editor
Conscience on Campus   Waldo Beach
The Prophetic Voice in Modern Fiction William R. Mueller
The Renewal of Hope   Howard Clark Kee
Christianity and Communism Today   John C. Bennett
The Christian as a Doctor

James T. Stephens and Edward LeRoy Long, Jr.
Christianity and the Scientist   Ian G. Barbour
The Art of Christian Doubt   Fred Denbeaux
The Christian as a Journalist   Richard T. Baker